Software Agreements Line by Line

A Detailed Look at Software Agreements and How to Draft Them to Meet Your Needs

2ND EDITION

Michael R. Overly and James R. Kalyvas

ASPATORE

For additional copies or customer service inquiries, please e-mail west.customer.service@thomson.com.

ISBN 978-0-314-29467-8

Mat #41911506

ASPATORE

Aspatore Books, a Thomson Reuters business, exclusively publishes C-Level executives and partners from the world's most respected companies and law firms. Each publication provides professionals of all levels with proven business and legal intelligence from industry insiders—direct and unfiltered insight from those who know it best. Aspatore Books is committed to publishing an innovative line of business and legal titles that lay forth principles and offer insights that can have a direct financial impact on the reader's business objectives.

ACKNOWLEDGMENT

We would like to thank our many clients for the privilege of assisting them with their critical technology transactions for over two decades and for their generosity in sharing with us their insights and best practices on how to achieve success with technology initiatives. We would also like to recognize our many colleagues at Foley & Lardner LLP that challenge and help us every day to find new ways to bring value to our clients.

DEDICATION

To Amy and Emma: The light at the end of the tunnel.

– Michael R. Overly

To Mom and Dad. Thank you!

– James R. Kalyvas

CONTENTS

Foreword

In this second edition, we have included updates in every chapter to reflect changes in contracting practices, new risks, and current trends. In particular, over the past few years, there have been three alarming trends in the software industry. These trends have fundamentally changed the risks presented in many software licensing engagements. Each is discussed below.

Buyer Beware

It is an unfortunate sign of the times that some vendors have become almost predatory in their approach to their customer relationships and the products they provide. We have seen vendors in multiple transactions with various customers under-represent the fees involved, particularly implementation fees, to "get the business," only to greatly increase those fees, sometimes up to double, through change requests and other means. In other cases, vendors have allowed customers to deploy software products knowing they have fundamental bugs or that they intend to sunset the product in the near future. Still other vendors conduct incredibly invasive and protracted audits of their customers in an effort to identify the smallest infraction in use of their products so that they can not only generate further revenue, but also shift what can be excessive audit costs to the customer. Finally, we have seen a steep increase in the number of software transactions end in disputes and early termination because the vendor simply could not perform.

Vendor Risk Aversion

Another disturbing trend is the growing resistance on the part of vendors to assume any real risk for their solutions (whether the failure or liability is caused by their product, people, or processes), shifting almost the entire burden of such risks onto the customer. Concessions and protections most vendors would have readily provided just a few years ago are now being rejected or have become far more difficult to negotiate. In some instances, even in very large engagements, vendors are essentially providing their products on an as-is basis, with virtually no meaningful protections for the customer. All too often, we will receive a call from a customer who has suffered extreme cost overruns or who has implemented a product that never provided the functionality or performance the vendor promised in its marketing materials. In many of those cases, the vendor contract is so one-sided that the customer has little or no remedy, other than to suffer the loss of its investment. In some instances, the contract cannot be terminated for breach because the vendor has not promised anything. In those engagements, the customer may end up paying year after year for a product that never worked properly.

The Constantly Changing Contract

Finally, many vendors are moving key parts of their contracts to the cloud, merely referencing them through URLs that can change at any time, without notice, and without any ability of the customer to object. These moving parts go to the heart of the transaction: product functionality, service level obligations, and support and maintenance services. While the body of the agreement may be fixed, these critical elements are subject to change at the vendor's whim. In contrast, the customer's obligations are fixed and cannot be varied. The customer must make an irrevocable commitment to purchase a product, but key elements of the vendor's obligations are not fixed. Changes could occur that greatly impact the utility of the deal and product to the customer. In one case, a hospital implemented a multi-million-dollar medical information system only to discover a year later that one of the key areas of functionality in the system was going to be dropped. The customer had no grounds to object under the agreement.

In view of these and other trends in the industry designed to shift risk to the customer, businesses must be more vigilant than in the past when negotiating their software agreements and ensure they understand the risks they are absorbing. While ten years ago, some businesses were comfortable viewing select software vendors as "partners," that term is infrequently earned by vendors today. This is not to say that all vendors are engaging in these practices. Many continue to view their customers as truly important to them and desire long-term relationships. They understand the pressures customers are under and that budgets are tight in the current economic environment. They work to ensure reasonable outcomes for both parties. Those vendors should be sought out. Unfortunately, they may not be available in all potential transactions. In cases in which the vendor is not willing to stand behind its offering, the concept of "buyer beware" cannot be over-emphasized.

One of the most important means of mitigating risk and realizing the benefits your business is paying for in the current vendor contracting environment is to maintain negotiating leverage at all times. The use of competitive processes, such as a request for proposals, can ensure vendors understand they are competing for the business. Avoid allowing vendors to believe they "have the deal" until an acceptable contract, including key relationship terms, is executed. All too often, customers seriously undermine their negotiating leverage by communicating to vendors that they have the solution the customer is looking for and that "the business has decided to move forward." We have seen time and time again that the customer who is willing to walk away from a transaction, rather than assume undue risk, is the customer who is able to achieve business terms and protections against risk that facilitate achieving their business objectives. While it may be difficult to avoid becoming too invested in a deal, doing so seldom results in optimal results.

Throughout this latest edition of our book, we have included notes and suggestions designed to mitigate the risks described above.

Michael R. Overly and James R. Kalyvas
Los Angeles 2015

Introduction

Successful use of technology frequently dictates prosperity in today's marketplace. Every business, regardless of size or industry, depends on technology to remain competitive or to obtain a competitive advantage. Despite huge investments in technology, many organizations lack the specialized knowledge required to optimally structure their relationships with service, software, and equipment vendors, which are critical to the success of their technology initiatives.

Over the past twenty years, we have represented technology users in formulating and executing successful strategies for the licensing and implementation of software. From the outset of our involvement in structuring and negotiating software licensing transactions, we observed that the typical vendor software license had much less to do with the licensing of its technology than it did with the creation of multiple revenue streams flowing from the user to the vendor and the elimination or minimization of most forms of accountability from the vendor to the user. It is surprising to us not only how broadly accepted the standard vendor approach to software licensing is among the user community but, earlier in particular, how much resistance there was in the user community to challenging these standard vendor approaches to licensing. Nevertheless, clients we represent have for years challenged these standard approaches with considerable success.

Today, our best practice approach to technology transactions, including software licensing, has evolved from the experiences accumulated through thousands of transactions. Implementation of these best practice approaches to software licensing has provided our clients with the tools they need to manage their technology initiatives to success, and has significantly reduced the costs and business risks associated with such initiatives. Notwithstanding the benefits of a structured enterprise approach to software licensing, including the procurement process, structuring and negotiation of the transaction, and implementation of the software system, the vast majority of businesses today still procure technology utilizing standard vendor forms and making minor adjustments to selected terms. In recognition that not all software licensing transactions warrant a customized license, we have designed this book to provide a context-based discussion of relevant business issues and recommended language for use in the modification of the typical vendor software license.

To promote the utility of this book in your company's day-to-day assessment and review of software licenses, we have created a composite vendor-oriented license agreement, introduced in Chapter 1, to serve as a touchstone for discussion and analysis of issues. The composite vendor-oriented license agreement contains terms and conditions common to most types of software licenses, and it is used in transactions ranging from thousands to millions of dollars. We will utilize the composite agreement to highlight and discuss key issues that any user entering into a software license must address and to offer recommendations as to how relatively minor changes to the composite agreement can significantly improve the outcome of the software licensing negotiation from your perspective.

Of course, not all software licensing transactions have the same business significance, cost, or risks. Chapter 2 provides a framework for assessing key factors that will help you better structure your approach to a particular software licensing transaction.

Chapters 3, 4, and 5 identify and discuss key issues impacting software licensing transactions and provide guidance as to how best to approach the software license transaction based on your assessment of these issues. Particular attention is given to issues such as:

1. The scope of the license granted by the vendor to the user, restrictions on use of the software, and identification and minimization of fees;
2. The importance of user-developed software specifications and approaches to acceptance testing to ensure that the product delivered meets the business objectives identified in your business case supporting the transaction and delivers the promised functionality; and
3. That an adequate measure of vendor accountability is built into the agreement through a coordinated use of warranties, indemnities, and allocated liability.

Vendor accountability, in particular, is an area where the typical user practice is deficient. As discussed in detail in Chapter 5, vendor accountability is central to ensuring that the vendor's business interests require it to deliver on the promises it has made and that the vendor is not so insulated from liability that it can either require you to pay additional fees for legitimate corrective actions or choose to walk away rather than absorb the costs of correction.

Attention surrounding issues of confidentiality and security with regard to both your businesses' and your customers' data and key processes has increased exponentially in recent years. The distinction between confidentiality and security is sometimes blurred by both customers and vendors, and these issues are often inadequately addressed in software licenses. In Chapter 6, we discuss the protections licensees should require in their vendor agreements to ensure the licensee's sensitive data and information are held in confidence and adequately protected from authorized access, and we provide recommendations to help you in structuring diligence inquiries based on the criticality of the data and applicable confidentiality requirements surrounding the transaction.

In Chapter 7, we provide a framework for evaluating your software maintenance and support requirements. We also provide tips to help you obtain the appropriate level of maintenance and support for a particular transaction and avoid hidden costs related to receiving the entire spectrum of software enhancements, whether such enhancements are characterized as a patch, a correction, an update, a revision, a release, a version, or some other term.

In Chapter 8, we discuss various terms that can independently significantly affect the quality of your software license, but do not neatly aggregate under a single chapter heading, resulting in the tantalizing chapter title "Miscellaneous Licensing Provisions." Do not be misled by the title; this chapter discusses issues of critical importance to the meaning, risk allocations, and adaptability of your software license, including ownership of intellectual property, limitations of liability, and the impacts of a change of control at your software vendor. Finally, we discuss the importance of addressing in detail the concept of change within your enterprise—whether through merger, acquisition, or divestiture—and the ability to use the software with your business partners as dictated by your expanding and interactive business relations.

In Chapter 9, we advocate for the implementation of an enterprise information technology management process in which business processes and tools are used to create an enterprise-specific, best practice approach to software licensing and technology services procurement, structure and negotiation, and implementation. We discuss the business drivers supporting the use of a structured approach to software licensing in your organization and provide specific recommendations on how to implement such a process effectively.

The appendices provide additional background material for the reader. Appendix information includes Internet-related resources, a table cross-referencing specific provisions of the vendor form license agreement to the chapters in which they are discussed, and a glossary of key terms used throughout this book.

There are valuable nuggets of knowledge gathered through our involvement in billions of dollars of technology transactions over the years. We encourage you to find those ideas that you think can drive the highest value to your organization and put them in place on a fast track. After your initial successes, come back to the book to structure subsequent phases of improvement to software licensing in your organization.

While this book is primarily directed at the issues raised in licensing software for installation on the customer's own systems (i.e., locally installed software), the base concepts can be applied more broadly to cloud, subscription, and other forms of software licensing engagements. In those instances, however, additional terms relating to service levels, security, disaster recovery, etc., may be applicable and are beyond the scope of this book.

1

The Vendor License

In this chapter, we introduce the form vendor-oriented license agreement we will be working with for the remainder of the book. *This is not the form agreement or terms we recommend you accept; rather, it is the form agreement and terms you should expect.* The agreement contains terms and conditions common to almost every type of software license. While relatively brief, this type of license is used by vendors in transactions that range from a few thousand dollars to many millions of dollars, involving software applications that range from those that are merely incidental to the overall operation of the licensee's business to those that are business-critical. Developing an understanding of each of the provisions in the form license will provide the means for assessing the legal and business risks of most common licenses in use by vendors today. We urge you to become familiar with the content of the form license agreement before proceeding to the discussion in the remainder of the book.

Generally, licensors like to create multiple contracts to govern their relationships with customers. For example, in the context of a larger software licensing engagement, they may ask the licensee to sign a master professional services agreement, license agreement, and maintenance and support agreement. This practice should be avoided. It is in both parties' best interest to clearly define the entire relationship between them in a single agreement. A single agreement not only is easier to refer to, but also:

1. Avoids inconsistencies in the use of defined terms,
2. Ensures that the remedies are coordinated, and
3. Makes it easier for the licensee to manage the fees and costs owed to the licensor.

Such an approach also prevents the vendor from balkanizing its responsibilities. For example, in a larger software licensing engagement in which substantial professional services will be rendered to implement the software, it is critical that the vendor not be permitted to isolate the obligation to implement the software from the software license agreement. Doing so could potentially result in one of two negative outcomes. First, the implementation services could fail, leaving the customer with a license agreement it cannot terminate because the implementation services were separated from the vendor's obligation to provide a functioning system. Second, and a corollary to the first negative outcome, the implementation services could be performed perfectly, but the software contains a fundamental flaw. The customer may be able to terminate the license agreement because of the flaw, but would be unable to recover the substantial professional service fees paid to implement the non-functional software because each is addressed in a separate contract.

Under either scenario, the business is left without the system it contracted for and without a remedy that approaches compensating it for the entire impact of the loss. In smaller license agreements, vendors will attempt to achieve a result similar to the "separate agreement" model that vendors use in large transactions by way of online agreements referencing separate URLs, as we mentioned in the Foreword.

The single agreement approach is used in the form vendor agreement we will be discussing in this book.

Licensors will likely resist the concept of a single agreement by arguing the single-agreement approach makes their administration of the agreement extremely complicated because different individuals or departments are involved with different aspects of the agreement. Whether this is true or not, it is not a sufficient reason for the licensee to approach contracting in a way that could lead to inconsistencies and surprises. If the licensee stands firm on the single-agreement approach, the licensor will generally back down.

If the licensor refuses to utilize a single agreement, it becomes even more critical to ensure that:

1. Defined terms are used consistently across the various agreements;
2. The remedies and damage limits are consistent; and

3. Protections obtained in one agreement are not eliminated or weakened in other agreements.

Another important point is to include a "precedence provision" in *each* of the agreements. Such a provision specifies that in the event of a conflict between the license agreement and any of the other documents, the terms of the license agreement will govern. For example, "In the event of a conflict between the License Agreement, the Support Agreement, and the Service Agreement, the License Agreement shall take precedence."

A sample, or model, vendor-form agreement follows to illustrate these points. Becoming familiar with this agreement is essential to understanding the discussion in the remainder of the book.

SOFTWARE LICENSE, SUPPORT, AND MAINTENANCE AGREEMENT

This Software License, Support, and Maintenance Agreement ("Agreement") is made and entered into as of ________________, 20__ ("Reference Date"), by and between ________________ ("Vendor") and ________________ ("Customer").

In consideration of valuable consideration and the mutual promises herein contained, the parties agree as follows:

AGREEMENT

1. Definitions

The following terms, when used in this Agreement, shall have the following meanings:

1.1 "Server" shall mean the CPU, whether in a PC, server, or other device, configured to run the Licensed Software and process transactions.

1.2 "Equipment" shall mean the computer and telecommunications hardware listed in Exhibit "A" (Equipment and Licensed Software Listing and Fee/Payment Schedule).

1.3 "Licensed Software" shall mean the object code version of the computer programs to be provided by Vendor to Customer, as listed in Attachment "A" (Equipment and Licensed Software Listing and Fee/Payment Schedule).

1.4 "Documentation" shall mean Vendor's then current documentation for the Licensed Software.

1.5 "Open Source Software" shall mean any software, programming, or other intellectual property that is subject to the GNU General Public License, GNU Library General Public License, Artistic License, BSD license, Mozilla Public License, or any similar license, including, but not limited to, those licenses listed at www.opensource.org/licenses.

1.6 "Third Party Software" shall mean software, including Open Source Software, licensed from third parties and included in the Licensed Software.

2. Software License

2.1 *License Grant.* Subject to the terms and conditions of this Agreement, Vendor grants to Customer a non-exclusive, non-transferable, limited license to use the Licensed Software solely for Customer's internal business purposes, subject to the number of licensed concurrent users. Customer may make one copy of the Licensed Software in machine-readable form for back-up and archival purposes only. Customer shall reproduce and include the copyright, trade secret, or other restrictive and proprietary notices and markings from the original on all copies. All copies will be subject to the terms of this Agreement.

2.2 *License Software Use Restrictions.* Customer's use of the Licensed Software shall be subject to the following restrictions:

A. The Licensed Software shall be used solely for Customer's internal business purposes and only by authorized concurrent users;

B. Customer shall not cause the Licensed Software in any way to be disassembled, decompiled, or reverse-engineered, nor shall any attempt to do so be undertaken or permitted;

C. Customer shall not make the Licensed Software available for access or use by any person or entity other than Customer's employees, including, but not limited to, acting as a service bureau;

D. Customer shall not upload, post, publish, or create derivative works of the Licensed software; and

E. Copy, translate, port, modify, or make derivative works of the Licensed Software.

2.5 *Ownership.* This Agreement does not grant to Customer any ownership interest in the Licensed Software. Rather, Customer has a license to use the Licensed Software as provided in this Agreement. Customer hereby agrees and acknowledges that Vendor owns all right, title, and interest in the Licensed Software, and Customer will not contest those rights or engage in any conduct contrary to those rights. Any copy, modification, revision, enhancement, adaptation, translation, or derivative work of or created from the Software made by or at the direction of Customer shall be owned solely and exclusively by Vendor, as shall all patent rights, copyrights, trade secret rights, trademark rights, and all other proprietary rights, worldwide (all of the foregoing rights taken together being referred to collectively herein as "Intellectual Property Rights") therein and thereto. Customer hereby irrevocably assigns and transfers to Vendor all of Customer's Intellectual Property Rights in the foregoing.

2.6 *Feedback.* Customer may provide suggestions, comments, or other feedback (collectively, "Feedback") to Vendor with respect to its products and services, including the Licensed Software. Feedback is voluntary. Provider may use Feedback for any purpose without obligation of any kind. Customer hereby irrevocably assigns and transfers to Vendor all of Customer's Intellectual Property Rights in the Feedback.

2.7 *Copyright.* The Licensed Software contains material that is protected by United States copyright law and trade secret law, and by international treaty provisions. All rights not granted to Vendor by this Agreement are expressly reserved by Vendor. Customer shall not remove any proprietary notice of Vendor from any copy of the Licensed Software.

2.8 *Delivery.* Vendor will deliver the object code version of the Licensed Software to Customer within five (5) days of the Reference Date. Customer will be deemed to have accepted the Licensed Software on delivery.

2.9 *Third Party Software.* To the extent any Third Party Software is provided with the Licensed Software, Customer agrees to comply with the terms and conditions of the applicable third party licenses associated with the Third Party Software, in addition to the terms and restrictions contained in this Agreement. All relevant licenses for the Third Party Software are provided at www.vendor.com/thirdpartysoftware. Customer's use of the Licensed Software shall be deemed its acceptance of the third party licenses. VENDOR MAKES NO WARRANTY OF ANY KIND, WHETHER EXPRESS OR IMPLIED, WITH REGARD TO ANY THIRD PARTY SOFTWARE. ALL THIRD PARTY SOFTWARE IS PROVIDED "AS-IS," WITHOUT WARRANTIES OF ANY KIND BY VENDOR. IN NO EVENT WILL VENDOR BE LIABLE TO LICENSEE OR ANY THIRD PARTY FOR ANY DIRECT, INDIRECT, PUNITIVE, EXEMPLARY, INCIDENTAL, SPECIAL, OR CONSEQUENTIAL DAMAGES ARISING OUT OF THE THIRD PARTY SOFTWARE, EVEN IF VENDOR HAS BEEN ADVISED OF THE POSSIBILITY OF SUCH DAMAGES OR LOSSES.

2.10 *Aggregated Data.* Vendor shall have the right to use all aggregated and statistical data arising from Customer's use of the Licensed Software. All such information may be used by Vendor for any purpose.

2.11 *Audit.* During the term of this Agreement and for one year thereafter, Vendor may audit Customer's use of the Licensed Software ("Audit"). An Audit may include, without limitation, the inspection and review of computers or servers on which the Licensed Software has been installed or hosted, and records, procedures, or business practices that relate to Customer's performance under and compliance with the terms of this Agreement. Vendor, its designees and agents, and any third party licensors may conduct such audits. They shall provide Customer at least five calendar days' advance notice of an Audit. Customer will reasonably cooperate in the Audit. The cost of the Audit shall be borne by Vendor, unless the Audit reveals a material breach of this Agreement by Customer (including any use of the Licensed Software in excess of the rights granted hereunder or failure to pay fees due), in which case the reasonable cost of the Audit shall be paid by Customer. In the event Customer has failed to pay all fees due, Customer shall immediately pay such fees, plus interest at the maximum rate permitted by law. If Customer has used the Licensed Software in excess of the rights granted hereunder, Customer shall pay all applicable additional license fees at Vendor's then current rates. Payment of the foregoing fees is in addition to and cumulative of all other rights of Vendor under this Agreement.

3. Support and Maintenance

3.1 *General Obligations.* Subject to Customer's payment of the annual support fees set forth in Exhibit A, Vendor will provide Customer with reasonable telephone support regarding use and operation of the Licensed Software during Vendor's normal hours of support, all as further described in Vendor's then current Support Services Program, available at www.vendor.com/SupportServices. Only the current version of the software will be supported. Customer must install all new versions of the Licensed Software within thirty (30) days of receipt. Vendor reserves the right to charge Customer for support issues that could have been resolved by reference to the Documentation or arise from the Customer's negligence, misuse of the Licensed Software, and issues relating to third party equipment and software. Vendor will provide Customer with any new versions of the Licensed Software that Vendor in its sole discretion makes available to its other licensees at no charge.

3.2 *Support Term and Fees.* Maintenance and support will automatically renew for additional one- (1-) year periods unless either party gives the other party written notice of its intent to not renew at least thirty (30) days prior to the expiration of the then current term. Vendor may increase support fees at any time on thirty (30) days' prior notice to Customer.

4. Term

This Agreement shall be effective as of the Reference Date and shall continue in effect unless terminated earlier in accordance with this Agreement.

5. Fees and Payment

5.1 *License and Support Fees.* Customer shall pay the license, support, and other fees set forth in Exhibit A. All fees paid hereunder are non-cancellable and nonrefundable. In the event of any failure to pay fees due, Customer shall reimburse Vendor for all costs of collection, including attorneys' fees.

5.2 *Taxes; Telecommunications Charges.* Customer shall pay all federal, state, and local taxes, government fees, and other similar amounts that are levied or imposed on the Charges, this Agreement, or the transactions hereunder, including sales, use, excise, and value added taxes. Customer shall pay for all telecommunication and carrier charges arising from its use of the Services or the transmittal of information to or from Vendor.

5.3 *Travel and Other Expenses.* Customer shall reimburse Vendor for all reasonable travel, living, and other out-of-pocket expenses incurred by Vendor personnel in connection with this Agreement.

5.4 *Payment.* Unless provided otherwise herein, Customer agrees to pay all amounts due under this Agreement within thirty (30) days after the date of invoice. Past due amounts will bear interest of one and one-half percent (1-1/2%) per month from the due date or the highest rate permitted by law if less. All payments made under this Agreement shall be nonrefundable, except as specifically provided otherwise in this Agreement.

6. Confidentiality

Customer shall treat the Licensed Software, related documentation, and all other information provided by Vendor in the strictest confidence and shall not reveal such information to anyone other than Customer's own employees.

7. Limited Warranty

7.1 *Licensed Software.* Vendor warrants that the Licensed Software shall perform substantially in accordance with the documentation for a period of ninety (90) days after the Reference Date (the "Initial Warranty Period"). Customer shall provide written notice of any warranty failure to Vendor not less than five (5) days prior to the end of the Initial Warranty Period. Such notice shall specify with particularity the nature of any such failure. Vendor shall not be responsible for any errors or nonconformities in the Licensed Software resulting from Customer's misuse, negligence, or modification of the Licensed Software.

7.2 *Services.* Vendor warrants that all services provided by Vendor to Customer under this Agreement shall be performed in a workmanlike manner.

8. Disclaimer of Warranties

VENDOR EXPRESSLY DISCLAIMS ALL WARRANTIES, EXPRESS AND IMPLIED, INCLUDING, BUT NOT LIMITED TO, THE IMPLIED WARRANTIES OF MERCHANTABILITY AND FITNESS FOR A PARTICULAR PURPOSE. VENDOR DOES NOT WARRANT THAT THE PRODUCTS WILL MEET CUSTOMER'S REQUIREMENTS, THAT THE LICENSED SOFTWARE IS COMPATIBLE WITH ANY PARTICULAR HARDWARE OR SOFTWARE PLATFORM, OR THAT THE OPERATION OF THE LICENSED SOFTWARE WILL BE UNINTERRUPTED OR ERROR-FREE, OR THAT DEFECTS IN THE LICENSED SOFTWARE WILL BE CORRECTED. THE ENTIRE RISK AS TO THE RESULTS AND PERFORMANCE OF THE LICENSED SOFTWARE IS ASSUMED BY CUSTOMER. FURTHERMORE, VENDOR DOES NOT WARRANT OR MAKE ANY REPRESENTATION REGARDING THE USE OR THE RESULTS OF THE USE OF THE LICENSED SOFTWARE OR RELATED DOCUMENTATION IN TERMS OF THEIR CORRECTNESS, ACCURACY, QUALITY, RELIABILITY, APPROPRIATENESS FOR A PARTICULAR TASK OR APPLICATION, CURRENTNESS, OR OTHERWISE. NO ORAL OR WRITTEN INFORMATION OR ADVICE GIVEN BY VENDOR OR VENDOR'S AUTHORIZED REPRESENTATIVES SHALL CREATE A WARRANTY OR IN ANY WAY INCREASE THE SCOPE OF WARRANTIES PROVIDED IN THIS AGREEMENT.

9. Limitation of Liability

IN NO EVENT SHALL VENDOR BE LIABLE TO CUSTOMER OR ANY THIRD PARTY FOR ANY INCIDENTAL OR CONSEQUENTIAL DAMAGES (INCLUDING, WITHOUT LIMITATION, INDIRECT, SPECIAL, PUNITIVE, OR EXEMPLARY DAMAGES FOR LOSS OF BUSINESS, LOSS OF PROFITS, BUSINESS INTERRUPTION, LOSS OF DATA, OR LOSS OF BUSINESS INFORMATION) ARISING OUT OF OR CONNECTED IN ANY WAY WITH USE OF OR INABILITY TO USE THE LICENSED SOFTWARE, OR FOR ANY CLAIM BY ANY OTHER PARTY, EVEN IF VENDOR HAS BEEN ADVISED OF THE POSSIBILITY OF SUCH DAMAGES. VENDOR'S TOTAL LIABILITY TO CUSTOMER FOR ALL DAMAGES, LOSSES, AND CAUSES OF ACTION (WHETHER IN CONTRACT, TORT [INCLUDING NEGLIGENCE], OR OTHERWISE) SHALL NOT EXCEED THE PURCHASE PRICE. THE LIMITATIONS PROVIDED IN THIS SECTION SHALL APPLY EVEN IF ANY OTHER REMEDIES FAIL OF THEIR ESSENTIAL PURPOSE.

10. Indemnification

Customer shall defend, indemnify, and hold Vendor and its directors, officers, agents, employees, members, subsidiaries, and affiliates from and against any claim, action, proceeding, liability, loss, damage, cost, or expense (including, without limitation, attorneys' fees), arising out of or in connection with Customer's use of the Licensed Software.

11. Default; Termination

11.1 *Termination Upon Event of Default.* If any party:

A. Breaches any covenant, obligation, representation, or warranty under this Agreement (other than those described in paragraph B below, and fails to cure such breach: (1) within seven (7) days after its receipt of written notice thereof from the other party for any such breach involving a failure to pay any amounts due hereunder, it being agreed that any such breach shall be a material breach hereof, or (2) within thirty (30) days after its receipt of written notice thereof from the other party of any other such breach; or

B. Breaches any covenant, obligation, representation, or warranty under this Agreement relating to confidentiality, scope of use, use restrictions, or proprietary rights (including Intellectual Property Rights), it being agreed that any such breach shall be a material breach hereof; or

C. Voluntarily or involuntarily suspends, terminates, winds up, or liquidates its business; becomes subject to any bankruptcy or insolvency proceeding under applicable law; or becomes insolvent or subject to direct control by a trustee, receiver, or similar authority, then, upon the occurrence of such event (each, an "Event of Default"), the other party may terminate this Agreement by giving notice of such termination to the defaulting party and/or may exercise any and all other rights and remedies under this Agreement, at law, or in equity.

11.2 *Effect of Termination.* On and after the effective date of any termination of this Agreement, Customer shall cease all use of the Software. Within ten (10) days of the effective date of termination of this Agreement by either party, Customer shall, at its own expense, return to Vendor (or destroy) all documentation and other tangible materials provided by Vendor hereunder in connection with the Licensed Software, together with a certificate signed by one of Customer's officers attesting to such return or destruction. Each party shall remain liable to the other party for all charges, obligations, and liabilities that accrue or arise under this Agreement from any event, occurrence, act, omission, or condition transpiring or existing prior to the effective date of such termination.

11.3 *Limitation of Actions.* Customer shall not bring any action against Vendor arising out of or related to this Agreement or the subject matter hereof more than one (1) year after the occurrence of the event that gave rise to such action.

12. Equitable Relief

Customer acknowledges and agrees that Vendor will be irreparably injured if the provisions of Sections 3 (Software License) and 7 (Confidentiality) are not capable of being specifically enforced, and agree that Vendor shall be entitled to equitable remedies for any breach of Sections 3 and 7,[1] in addition to, and cumulative with, any legal rights or remedies, including the right to damages.

---

[1] Sections 3 and 7.

13. Independent Contractor

Vendor acknowledges that it is at all times acting as an independent contractor under this Agreement and except as specifically provided herein, not as an agent, employee, joint venturer, or partner of Customer.

14. Notices

Any notices required or permitted to be given hereunder by either party to the other shall be in writing and shall be deemed duly given or made if delivered: (1) by personal delivery; (2) by electronic facsimile with confirmation sent by United States first class registered or certified mail, postage prepaid, return receipt requested; (3) by bonded courier or by a nationally recognized overnight delivery company; or (4) by United States first class registered or certified mail, postage prepaid, return receipt requested, in each case, addressed to the parties as follows (or to such other addresses as the parties may request in writing by notice given pursuant to this Section):

If to Vendor:

____

____

If to Customer:

____

____

Notices shall be deemed received on the earliest of personal delivery; twenty-four (24) hours following deposit with a bonded courier or overnight delivery company; or seventy-two (72) hours following deposit in the US Mail as required herein.

15. Force Majeure

Vendor shall not be responsible for failures of its obligations under this Agreement to the extent that such failure is due to causes beyond Vendor's control, including, but not limited to, acts of God, war, acts of any government or agency thereof, fire, explosions, epidemics, quarantine restrictions, strikes, delivery services, telecommunication providers, labor difficulties, lockouts, embargoes, severe weather conditions, delay in transportation, or delay of suppliers or subcontractors.

16. Choice of Law

This Agreement shall be construed and enforced in accordance with the laws of the state of Florida.

17. Entire Agreement

This Agreement constitutes the entire agreement between the parties with respect to the subject matter hereof and supersedes all other prior and contemporary agreements, understandings, and commitments between the parties regarding the subject matter of this Agreement. This Agreement may not be modified or amended except by a written instrument executed by the parties. In particular, any provisions, terms, or conditions contained in Customer's Purchase Orders or other similar forms that are in any way inconsistent with or in addition to the terms and conditions of this Agreement shall not be binding upon Vendor.

18. Severability

If any provision of this Agreement is found to be invalid or unenforceable by any court, such provision shall be ineffective only to the extent that it is in contravention of applicable laws without invalidating the remaining provisions of the Agreement.

19. Assignment

Neither this Agreement nor any interest in this Agreement may be assigned by Customer without the prior express written approval of Vendor. Vendor may assign, pledge, mortgage, sell to a third party, or otherwise dispose of all or any portion of this Agreement, provided that such action shall not relieve Vendor of its obligations to Customer under this Agreement or reduce Customer's rights hereunder.

20. Waiver

All waivers under this Agreement shall be in writing to be effective. No failure or delay by a party to exercise any right it may have by reason of the default of the other party shall operate as a waiver of default or as a modification of this Agreement or shall prevent the exercise of any right of the non-defaulting party under this Agreement.

21. Headings

Headings used in this Agreement are provided for convenience only and shall not be used to construe meaning or intent.

22. Agreement Drafted by Both Parties

This Agreement is the result of arm's-length negotiations between the parties and shall be construed to have been drafted by all parties such that any ambiguities in this Agreement shall not be construed against either party.

23. Counterparts

This Agreement may be executed in one or more counterparts, each of which shall be deemed an original, and will become effective and binding upon the parties as of the Reference Date, at such time as all the signatories hereto have signed a counterpart of this Agreement.

24. Publicity

Customer agrees Vendor may issue a press release regarding this engagement, include Customer's names and trademarks in its marketing materials and customer lists, and otherwise publicly promote this engagement. Customer also agrees to participate in a case study regarding the License Software.

IN WITNESS WHEREOF, the parties hereto have caused this Agreement to be executed as of the date first above written.

Accepted by:

[Vendor] ______________________

____

Authorized Signature

____

Print Name

____

Title

Accepted by:

[Customer]_______________________

____

Authorized Signature

____

Print Name

____

Title

2

Checklist for Assessing Software Licenses

Developing a structured, consistent approach to the review of software license agreements will expedite the review process, assist in training contract negotiators and other relevant personnel, reduce overall costs, increase the likelihood of achieving your technology objectives on time and on budget, and ensure key issues are not overlooked. In this chapter, we provide a general checklist of key issues and questions to bear in mind when reviewing and negotiating license agreements. As a preliminary step, however, we present six critical questions that should be answered before review of the agreement is even begun.

The Six Critical Questions

Whenever we are presented with a new software license to review, we begin by asking the client six foundational questions. While each of these questions may seem basic, even self-evident, our experience has shown that few businesses take the time to think through these issues before entering into their licensing transactions. The answers to these questions will, in large part, dictate the type and depth of the revisions you will request to the vendor's agreement.

1. *Business Purpose/Goals*

What is the business reason for acquiring this application? That is, what are the goals the business expects to achieve in implementing this software (e.g., greater productivity, cost savings, interoperability with other systems, streamlining of business processes, new processing capabilities or functionality)? While this seems like a straightforward question, it is remarkable how many times the relevant business personnel cannot articulate a clear response.

We suggest that if a clear reason cannot be articulated, the decision to acquire the software should be reconsidered or, at least, delayed until the specific business goals of implementing the application can be identified. Since the implementation of any new application will present risk to the licensee, a strong business case should form the basis of the decision to acquire each new application, regardless of its relative cost.

2. *Criticality*

How critical is the application to the organization? Will the application provide an essential business function? The answer to this question will frequently drive the performance levels we will require from the vendor.

For example, suppose the application will be a client-facing (e.g., an application with which customers, clients, or business partners will interact) website. Spotty availability and poor response time would likely result in loss of customers and harm to the licensee's business reputation. To ensure that this critical website performs properly and that the vendor has a continuing interest in ensuring good performance, specific service levels and appropriate remedies should be included in the agreement.

3. *Fees and Costs*

What are the initial license, support, and implementation fees and the ongoing yearly costs of the application? While this is potentially the most obvious of the six foundational questions, it is often the least clearly considered.

For example, few business people look past the first year of the contract or the implementation period regarding fees. They carefully lock in pricing during the implementation phase of the agreement, but give virtually no thought to price protection in later years, when the licensee will have little negotiating leverage to obtain favorable rates.

4. *Implementation Time and Plan*

How long will it take to implement the software? The longer the implementation period, the greater the likelihood for cost overruns, delays, and other problems.

Transactions involving implementations running over many months require special provisions regarding project management, staffing, cost and expense tracking, progress reporting, etc. Though many clients believe they cannot prepare a detailed project plan until after a deal is signed, the more thought that is put into the development of an implementation plan before the agreement is signed, the greater the understanding by all parties of the work required, its timing, and its costs.

5. *Data Security and Regulatory Issues*

Data security issues must be understood with any new system—and the requirement for specific diligence on security issues is not just a best practice, but is now required by the standard of care. The issues of security and other elements of an implementation are further impacted by whether the licensee is operating in a regulated industry (e.g., financial services or health care) where its contracts must be reviewed to ensure regulatory issues are addressed.

For example, if the licensee is a financial institution, it may be under an obligation to include limits on vendor subcontracting, prohibiting the transmission of sensitive data offshore, including strong confidentiality and security obligations, permitting termination for regulatory compliance issues, etc. Even if the licensee is not, itself, a regulated entity, will any data be placed at risk that is regulated (e.g., personally identifiable data of customers or employees, credit card information, etc.)? If so, the agreement must be revised to include protections relating to legal compliance, compliance with the Payment Card Industry Data Security Standard, confidentiality, information security, etc.

6. *Intellectual Property Ownership*

Does the engagement contemplate the creation of any enhancements or modifications to the licensor's base software that the licensee desires to own? This may arise when the licensee is paying substantial development fees or when it desires to prevent the licensor (at least for a period) from immediately providing the enhancements to one of the licensee's competitors. Will the licensor be providing advice that affects the licensee's business processes and workflows? Most implementations of significant systems do result in workflow changes, and the guidance and documentation related to those changes involve intellectual property rights.

Having clear answers to these six foundational questions will help ensure the licensee's goals in its negotiations with the vendor will be achieved.

Basic Licensing Checklist

The following is a basic checklist of key issues and questions to be considered in almost every software licensing transaction:

- ☒ Has appropriate due diligence been conducted on this vendor? Depending on the size of the transaction, due diligence may range from site visits at other licensees and requests for financial data to simple Internet searches of trade publications for mentions of the vendor. Depending on the criticality of the software, diligence may be conducted on the vendor's development practices, including security testing of its products. Do not just check the box when conducting diligence on a vendor; ask tough and direct questions of the reference. Most references want to be helpful, as they know they will be on the other side asking for someone else's help someday.
- ☒ What is being licensed? Does the agreement clearly define the applications being licensed?
- ☒ Does the license agreement define what the software is supposed to do—not merely refer to the vendor's "then current documentation"?
- ☒ Does the licensee have any specific performance requirements for the software (e.g., the ability to interface with other systems, exchange data with other software, or achieve certain performance levels)? If so, are those requirements included in the agreement or an exhibit?
- ☒ Who is the "licensee"? Is "licensee" defined broadly enough to encompass all possible users of the software being licensed?
- ☒ What is the scope of the license? What are the limitations on the licensee's use of the software? Does the scope of the license include all intended uses of the software? Always take into account potential future changes in use (e.g., the need to purchase additional user licenses). Software is rarely used by any one "for internal business purposes only" in today's connected world.
- ☒ What fees are due under the agreement? What is the projected yearly cost of operating the software? Have all possible revenue streams been identified (e.g., license fee, support fee, interface fees, customization fees, professional service fees)? Are there limitations

on future fee increases? How are support fees calculated? Look for vague references to the vendor being able to charge "then current" time and materials rates for various services.

☒ What is the term of the license? Is this a perpetual license or a term license? If it is a term license, how is the agreement renewed?

☒ What is the expected useful life of this application to the licensee (e.g., how long does the licensee expect to be using this application)?

☒ If the licensee has unique specifications, interoperability requirements, or functionality for the software, have those specifications been expressly included in the agreement?

☒ Is the software subject to acceptance testing? If so, how will acceptance testing be conducted? What type of testing will be used (installation, prior to go-live, user testing, security testing, etc.)?

☒ How long will it take to implement the software? Is there a formal implementation plan? Does the implementation include objective milestones for the vendor to achieve? Are payments tied to those milestones or to the mere passage of time?

☒ Does the vendor place the source code for its software into escrow with a third party? Who is the escrow agent? Has a copy of the escrow agreement been provided for review? What are the licensee's rights in the event of a release of the source code?

☒ What warranties are provided? Are any special or unique warranties required for this application (performance in accordance with regulatory requirements like the Health Insurance Portability and Accountability Act, Gramm-Leach Bliley, etc.)? Are any items (e.g., third-party software) excluded from the warranties?

☒ What are the vendor's support obligations? Is there a separate support agreement, or, preferably, is support integrated into the license agreement? If this is a critical application, are there specific service levels for responding to support calls? How long is the vendor obligated to support the software?

☒ Will the vendor have access to any proprietary or confidential information of the licensee and/or its customers? If so, have appropriate confidentiality and security provisions been incorporated into the agreement?

☒ What indemnities has the vendor provided (intellectual property infringement, personal injury, damage to property, breach of confidentiality, etc.)?

- ☒ What is the limitation of liability? What types of damages are excluded or limited? What is the overall cap on liability? Is anything excluded from the limitation of liability (e.g., indemnity for intellectual property infringement, breach of confidentiality)? Who is protected by the limitation of liability (i.e., is the limitation of liability applicable only to the vendor or to both parties)?
- ☒ Can the licensee assign the agreement to a successor entity or an affiliate?
- ☒ Does the licensee currently intend or does it reasonably foresee in the future the need to outsource operation of this application to a third party or an affiliate serving as a technology provider?
- ☒ Does the agreement grant the vendor any rights in aggregated data arising from the licensee's use of the software?
- ☒ Does the agreement include any right to use the licensee's name or trademarks, make press releases, require participation in case studies, etc.?
- ☒ Are any elements of the agreement referenced through URLs?

The foregoing is not intended to be an exhaustive list of all potential issues, but rather a listing of some of the key issues and questions that should be explored in every transaction. The list should be viewed as an organic document. The reader should expand the list to include issues that are unique to its organization, as well as issues that it identifies as important based on its experiences in reviewing and negotiating its own software licenses. By making the list its own, the reader will have developed a valuable resource for its enterprise.

Develop a Licensing Knowledgebase

Over the years, your organization will develop certain approaches to its licensing transactions. It will identify its own key issues and learn from its mistakes. As discussed in the preceding section, some of that knowledge should be transferred to the licensing checklist your organization uses in evaluating new transactions.

Another important resource is the previous contracts your organization has negotiated. We suggest keeping copies of the original, unmodified version of each of your vendor agreements, as well as the negotiated, final version.

These copies should be stored in a readily accessible manner, preferably as part of an electronic document management system that permits easy retrieval when needed. This knowledgebase of prior agreements can prove invaluable when negotiating new agreements.

For example, if you are considering a new transaction involving the license of content for your company's website, it will be useful to quickly review the other similar agreements your company has entered into. Apart from identifying potential key terms for this type of transaction, your review will also provide information about what this vendor's competitors are willing to accept in similar transactions. Your review may also disclose that your company has a master agreement with this particular vendor and that no new agreement is even needed. Licensees should not overlook this valuable resource for their transactions.

Floating Contract Terms

As illustrated in Section 3.1[2] of the example vendor license agreement in Chapter 1, many vendors are moving key elements of their agreements to the cloud, making them available through URLs that can change at any time. These key elements may go to the heart of the value of the transaction: product description and functionality, service levels, support obligations, etc. The customer is bound to a contract that the vendor can change at will. There are several approaches to this problem of contract "float."

First, consider requesting that the various referenced web-based documents be printed out and attached as exhibits to the agreement. This would "fix" the agreement and prevent it from changing.

Second, if the vendor refuses to fix the documents by attaching them to the agreement, consider including a limitation that any changes to the documents will not materially diminish the protections and obligations existing in those documents as of the contract effective date (i.e., the vendor's obligations in the documents can improve, but cannot grow worse from the perspective of the customer).

If the vendor rejects both of these approaches, consider negotiating a termination right if a material, adverse change is made to one of the documents.

---

[2] Section 3.1.

This is hardly a perfect result, particularly when the customer is paying any material, upfront, one-time fees. If the customer pays $100,000 in professional service fees to implement the software, being able to terminate because the vendor has fundamentally changed one of the contract documents referenced through a URL would not be realistic. In such cases, the customer must also negotiate some form of prorated refund of those one-time fees.

For example, if there is a fundamental change in the contract documents, and the customer elects to terminate in, say, the first two years of the contract, the customer would receive a refund of all one-time fees, prorated over that two-year period. After the two-year period, the customer would still have a termination right, but there would be no refund of one-time fees. In all events, the customer would also be entitled to a prorated refund of any prepaid fees (e.g., an annual license fee).

3

Scope of License Fees, Audit Rights

In this chapter, we turn to the provisions of the form vendor license agreement, introduced in Chapter 1, relating to the license grant, scope of license, restrictions on use, and fees. These provisions are, without doubt, some of the most important in the entire agreement. They define the scope of the licensee's right to use the software and the fees to be paid for that use. Careful attention to these provisions will ensure that the licensee is able to use the software for all of its intended purposes, that it has identified all costs associated with using the software, and that it has negotiated protections to ensure those costs are adequately controlled in later years of the agreement.

In addition, we discuss the primary means vendors use to police licenses to their software: audit clauses. These clauses permit vendors to ensure their licensees are using their software within the limits of the licenses they have been granted. For example, if three copies of the software have been licensed, an audit may be used to confirm three and only three copies of the software are in use. Unfortunately, vendors are using these clauses aggressively to generate new revenue streams and without regard to the quality and duration of the client relationship. In this chapter, we present methods to ensure that audit rights are used appropriately to protect the interests of both parties.

The following sections of the form license agreement are discussed in this chapter:

- Section 1.3 (Definition of Licensed Software)
- Section 2.1 (License Grant)

- Section 2.2 (Licensed Software Use Restrictions)
- Section 2.11 (Audit)
- Section 5 (Fees and Payment)

Defining the Subject of the License

One of the first provisions to review in assessing any software license is the definition of the software being licensed, typically referred to as the "Software," the "Licensed Software," or the "Application." In the form vendor agreement, the term "Licensed Software" is used, and a definition is provided in Section 1.3.[3]

From the licensee's perspective, the definition of "Licensed Software" should be as broad as possible, encompassing all software applications being licensed and all updates, enhancements, versions, and releases. There are two main reasons for requiring this breadth. First, it will ensure that the license grant covers all of the foregoing and that there are no additional licensee fees for the updates, enhancements, and new releases. Second, the warranties, intellectual property indemnity, support services, and other obligations of the licensor under the agreement are usually tied to the "Licensed Software" or "Licensed Product," so the licensee would automatically gain the benefit of those protections for any new updates, versions, and releases of the software.

Consider the language provided in Section 1.3.[4] As written, this definition could be construed to include only the software in the form originally provided to the licensee. Any later update or new release of the software would not be included in the definition and, therefore, not subject to the warranties and other protections provided in the agreement.

To address this problem, the definition of "Licensed Software" should be revised as follows:[5]

---

[3] Unless stated otherwise, throughout the remainder of the book, all references to sections will be to the form vendor agreement provided in Chapter 1.

[4] Section 1.3.

[5] Suggested revisions to language in the vendor form agreement will be indicated by means of underlining and strikeouts.

Example Revision:

1.3 "Licensed Software" shall mean the object code version of the computer programs to be provided by Vendor to Customer, as listed in Attachment "A" (Equipment and Licensed Software Listing and Fee/Payment Schedule), including all updates, releases, bug fixes, and enhancements thereto provided by Vendor to Customer under this Agreement.

License Grant and Term

License Grant

The best license from the perspective of the licensee is the *broadest license*, one that enables use of the licensed software across the licensee's entire enterprise and by all users authorized by the licensee, including, without limitation, employees, agents (such as outsourcers, consultants, and independent contractors), and all other affiliated entities. Most licenses, however, are drafted in terms of allowing only the licensee to use the software. Depending on pricing, consider expanding the license to include all of the individuals and entities that must have access to and use of the software.

Some vendors may object to the inclusion of the licensee's affiliates in the license. One way to address this concern is attach a current list of the licensee's affiliates and limit future affiliates that may use the software to those entities in which the licensee owns at least a 50 percent interest. In many instances, this will be sufficient to gain the licensor's approval to add the licensee's affiliates as users of the software.

Attention should be given not only to the users who will have access to the software, but also to the licensed or permitted uses of the software. Most form vendor agreements are written in terms of allowing the licensee to use the software for "its internal purposes only" or similar highly restrictive language. Such a restriction will likely not encompass all of the licensee's intended uses for the software. A better, more encompassing approach is to draft the license in terms of permitting the licensee to use the software for "its business purposes."

As an example, a business licensed a piece of software for use in interacting better with its customers. The license in the agreement, however, limited use to the licensee's internal purposes and made no mention of use by the licensee's customers. Even though the entire purpose of the software was to service the licensee's customers, because the license did not call this out specifically, the vendor, as part of a later audit, required the licensee to pay greatly increased fees so that it could continue to use the software as was intended.

License Term

Licenses that permit the licensee to use the software for only a limited period, typically one to five years, are generally disfavored. This type of license is referred to as a "term license." Such a limitation will require the licensee to pay a new license fee upon expiration of the term to continue use of a product that may have become important, even critical, to its business operations. At that point, after several years have passed since the initial installation of the software, the licensee will have little leverage in its license "renewal" negotiations. Such term licenses are, however, becoming more popular, replacing "perpetual" licenses as the default. Perpetual licenses entitle the licensee to use the software for an unlimited time without paying an additional license fee, and they limit the relevance of "term" discussions to issues of maintenance and support.[6]

If a perpetual license cannot be negotiated or is inappropriate for a given transaction, the term license should be drafted in such a way that the licensee may, *at the licensee's discretion*, renew the license for a defined period of years. For example, the agreement could have an initial term of three years, and thereafter, the licensee may, at its option, renew the license for up to five consecutive one-year renewal terms. For further discussion on this approach to drafting term provisions, see Chapter 7.

The point of expanding the term through optional renewal terms is to ensure the licensee has the ability to use the software throughout its projected useful life. Useful life will vary from application to application. Approaches to software involving mobile technologies, for example, may change rapidly. In such cases, the useful life of an application may be only one to three years before alternate or better technology becomes available. In other cases, such as a business's records management system, the technology is relatively stable

[6] *See* the discussion of support and maintenance terms in Chapter 7.

and unlikely to change dramatically over time. In such cases, the useful life may be five to eight years or even longer.

Note that in the form vendor agreement, it is not possible to tell from the face of the document whether the license being granted is perpetual or term. This is a common problem found in many vendor form agreements. The licensee should ensure that the license is revised to reflect the type of license being purchased: perpetual or term.

In some instances, the parties will have negotiated for some software products to be licensed on a perpetual basis and other products to be licensed on a term basis. In such a circumstance, the parties must clearly define the products in each category. This is typically done in an exhibit to the agreement (e.g., an order form) that lists the specific applications being licensed.

The following illustrates potential revisions to the limited license grant provided in the form vendor agreement:

Example Revision:

2.1 License Grant. Subject to the terms and conditions of this Agreement, Vendor grants to Customer a <u>world-wide</u>, non-exclusive, non-transferable <u>(except as provided herein)</u>,[7] ~~limited~~ license to use the Licensed Software solely for Customer's ~~internal~~ business purposes~~, subject to the number of licensed concurrent users~~. <u>For purposes of this Section, the term "Customer" shall include Customer and its affiliates and their respective employees and authorized contractors and agents.</u> Customer may make <u>a reasonable number of</u> copies ~~one copy~~ of the Licensed Software in machine-readable form for <u>disaster recovery,</u> backup and archival purposes only. Customer shall reproduce and include the copyright, trade secret, or other restrictive and proprietary notices and markings from the original on all copies. All copies will be subject to the terms of this Agreement.

License Restrictions

Every license agreement includes a list of restrictions or limits on the licensee's use of the software. Most of these exceptions are generally acceptable to

[7] *See* discussion of assignment in Chapter 8.

licensees. They relate, in large part, to unauthorized modification and distribution of the software, removal of the vendor's proprietary notices (e.g., copyright and trademark notices), reverse engineering, and the licensee's use of the software to serve as a service bureau for unrelated third parties. Two of these restrictions bear further discussion: reverse engineering and service bureaus.

Most commercial software developers treat the source code to their products as their most valuable proprietary information. They protect this information at all costs and make it available to their licensees only in the event of bankruptcy[8] or other unusual circumstances (e.g., the vendor elects to discontinue support for the product). Absent one of the foregoing circumstances, only the object code version of the software is delivered to the licensee.

To prevent the licensee from potentially reverse engineering or decompiling the object code to obtain the source code, licensors include strict prohibitions in their license agreements against such activities. In general, these prohibitions are entirely appropriate and necessary to protect the licensor's intellectual property rights.

There are, however, circumstances under which a licensee may need the ability to reverse engineer the software. This need typically arises when the licensee desires to interface the licensed software with another application or system. In such cases, the licensee will request the application programming interface (API) from the licensor to create the interface. If the licensor refuses to provide the information (potentially because the licensor desires to charge a substantial fee to create the interface itself), the licensee may have the right under the law to reverse engineer the software for the sole purpose of obtaining the necessary interface information. To protect this right, the licensor's prohibition against reverse engineering must be qualified with the licensee's right to engage in such activities to the extent permitted under applicable law.

"No service bureau" provisions are common in software licenses and ordinarily do not pose a substantial restriction on the licensee's use of the software. Keep in mind, however, that in some circumstances, the ability of a licensee to serve as a service bureau for its affiliates or other related businesses is critical. As such, this issue should be carefully considered in every license agreement. Ask

[8] *See* discussion of escrow provisions in Chapter 8.

the question, "Will we need the ability to process the data of any other entities?" If so, the provision should be revised specifically to permit the licensee to serve as a service bureau for those entities.

Example Revision:

2.2 License Software Use Restrictions. Except as permitted in this Agreement, Customer's use of the Licensed Software shall be subject to the following restrictions:

A. The Licensed Software shall be used solely for Customer's ~~internal~~ business purposes ~~and only by authorized concurrent users~~;

B. Customer shall not cause the Licensed Software in any way to be disassembled, decompiled, or reverse engineered~~, except to the extent permitted by applicable law,~~ nor shall any attempt to do so be undertaken or permitted;

C. Customer shall not make the Licensed Software available for access or use by any person or entity other than Customer's employees and authorized contractors and agents, including, but not limited to, acting as a service bureau. Notwithstanding the foregoing, Customer may serve as a service bureau for its affiliates; and

E. Copy, translate, port, modify, or make derivative works of the Licensed Software.

License Fees and Costs

License Fees

Software is typically licensed and priced on a specific metric (e.g., enterprise, named users, concurrent users, seats, or devices [*see* descriptions below]). The scope of the use restrictions that apply to a particular metric will limit the licensee's ability to, and impact the price of expanding use of, the licensed software. Thus, it is important to consider the licensee's future needs regarding the software and to provide for the licensee's ability to expand use of the software while the licensee's negotiation position is at its strongest (e.g., locking in the fees to add users or facilities during, at minimum, the first few years of the license term).

The following are the types of licenses most frequently encountered:

"Enterprise" provides the broadest license, but likely will be extremely expensive because fees are based on the size of the licensee's total enterprise. The term "enterprise" can be defined to apply to a single facility or to all facilities within an organization, but the license will still likely be more expensive than if the fee were calculated using one of the other metrics discussed below. An enterprise license should be considered for applications that will have broad and frequent use throughout the organization, such as a scheduling program or an e-mail product. For less ubiquitous products, an enterprise license is still valuable if it can be achieved without paying a significant premium over pricing that is calculated using other metrics. An enterprise license can also be simulated by simply expanding the definition of "licensee" to include all of the licensee's entities (*see* example revisions to Section 2.1,[9] above).

"Named Users" usually means the total number of specific types of users who are allowed to access the software, regardless of whether they are concurrently using the software. In these types of arrangements, the license should include language permitting the licensee to change the names of authorized users on notice to the vendor.

"Concurrent Users" usually means the number of users and devices that can simultaneously access the software. This type of limitation was once very popular but is less common today.

"Seats" usually refers to a total number of unique workstations through which the software can be accessed. The seats are paid for regardless of use. *"Devices"* usually means the software may be used only on specific hardware devices. If software is licensed for a particular server, a provision should be included permitting the licensee to change the designated server on notice to the vendor. This important right will ensure the licensee's ability to upgrade its equipment and to move the software to a "hot site" in the event of an emergency.

"Server" refers to the number of servers on which the software may be installed. These provisions can be profoundly complex. They may limit use

[9] Section 2.1.

to servers with only a certain number of cores and prohibit the use of virtual machines. The definition of "server" has been the subject of many disputes between vendors and their licensees. All such provisions should be carefully reviewed by the licensee's technology staff and legal counsel to ensure the limitations are workable within the licensee's environment and permit use as the licensee intends.

The type of metric used in a particular license will have important cost and scope of use implications. If defined properly, a "Concurrent User" license will generally be more cost-effective than a "Named Users" license or a "Seat" based license because the fee is more closely related to actual use. Keep in mind the scope of use restrictions that apply to a particular metric will limit the licensee's ability to use the software and impact the price of expanding use of the software. It is important to consider future expansion in use of the software at the time the license is negotiated and to provide for rights to such expansion (and any costs) in the agreement, when the licensee's negotiating position is at its strongest. For example, if there is a concurrent user limitation in the agreement, consider adding language regarding the cost of adding users (require discounts if blocks of users are added at the same time). The cost of additional users should be fixed for at least the first few years of the agreement. Thereafter, it may be possible to negotiate a yearly cap on fee increases (e.g., Consumer Price Index [CPI] or CPI plus 3 percent to 6 percent) for an additional two to three years.

If any third-party software will be provided by the licensor, the licensee should always request copies of the applicable license agreements and specifically inquire whether any concurrent user or other limitations exist on the use of the third-party software. It is possible, for example, that despite a broad license being obtained to use the licensor's main product, a scope-of-use limitation on a critical third-party product will act to limit the licensee's overall use of the system. Of course, the licensor should be required to identify specifically any additional fees associated with the third-party software in an exhibit to the license agreement.

Costs, Expenses, and Taxes

Unqualified statements requiring the licensee to pay all amounts billed by the licensor should be avoided. Invoices are the subject of frequent disputes.

Provisions such as the one provided in the vendor form agreement should be modified to include the concept of "disputed payments." In addition, the licensee's time for payment of an invoice should run from the date of receipt of the invoice, not the date the invoice is printed. Several days could lapse between the time the invoice is printed and the date on which it is sent to the licensee. If we add to that delay the time it takes the licensee to receive the invoice through the mail, a week or more may be lost. This could leave the licensee with little time to process the invoice and send payment to the licensor before interest will start accruing. If the vendor refuses to revise the agreement so that the time for payment runs from receipt of the invoice, the period for payment should be increased to allow for delays in processing and mailing on the vendor's side (e.g., increase the thirty-day payment period to forty-five days).

Section 5.4[10] of the form license shows a common trend in license agreements in which the vendor makes all fees non-refundable—even if the vendor fails to perform. Licensees should reject all provisions that make payments "non-refundable." Such provisions could literally permit licensors to retain license fees even if they never deliver the purchased software. If removal of this language is not possible, the language should be qualified to make clear it does not preclude the recovery of fees in the form of damages in the event of a dispute (e.g., "all fees are non-refundable (except in the form of damages)").

Travel and living expenses can quickly accumulate and amount to a significant percentage of the overall fees to be paid under the agreement. Prudent licensees will insist that controls be included in the agreement to require the licensor to obtain the licensee's approval before incurring these types of expenses. In some instances, the licensee may require the licensor to comply with the licensee's corporate travel policy, which may be attached to the agreement as an exhibit. An example travel provision follows:

Example Provision:

Travel and Living Expenses. Unless agreed otherwise, Vendor shall utilize Los Angeles[11] area personnel ("Local Personnel") whenever possible to minimize travel and living expenses incurred. Travel and living expenses

[10] Section 5.4.

[11] Insert licensee's location.

charged to Customer under this Agreement shall be consistent with Customer's current Travel and Living Policy, attached as Exhibit "__" (Travel and Living Policy). In particular, all commercial air travel shall be coach class. Receipts or reasonable evidence thereof is required for commercial travel, car rental, parking, and lodging. When Vendor employees visit more than one client on the same trip, the expenses incurred are apportioned in relation to time spent with each client. Vendor shall obtain Customer's prior written approval, which shall not be unreasonably withheld, before incurring any expenses exceeding, in the aggregate, One Thousand Dollars ($1,000.00). Vendor shall use commercially reasonable efforts to make airline reservations sufficiently in advance of the travel date to obtain the lowest airfare.

In some states, sales tax can be avoided by requiring the licensor to deliver the software and related documentation electronically, without any physical media. Most vendors are willing to cooperate in making delivery electronically. Licensees should review the laws of their particular states regarding taxation of software licenses. If this applies in your state, the following provision should be added to the license: "To the extent practicable, the Vendor shall deliver the Licensed Software and Documentation to Customer by electronic transmission." The agreement should also mention the format in which the software will be delivered.

Beware of omnibus tax clauses that make the licensee responsible for not only sales and use taxes, but also other, vague amounts for "government fees," "charges," and other undefined amounts. The licensee should be responsible for true sales, use, and other similar taxes based on the license it is receiving. Vague terms should be eliminated. Also, be cautious of references to foreign taxes, which may be hard to predict and calculate. Many vendors are now using offshore staffing for their projects. The use of this staffing may result in various foreign taxes. As an initial approach, references to foreign taxes should be removed. If that is not possible, the vendor should be required to identify clearly the exact amount of all such taxes in the relevant order document prior to purchase.

Overall Cost Control

Vendors have many ways to derive revenue from their license transactions. In many instances, the number of revenue streams that may flow from a particular agreement will be difficult to determine. One of the best ways to ensure the vendor has clearly disclosed all possible fees and costs associated with use of the software is to include language that excludes all fees that are not identified. *See* the new Section 5.5[12] provided in the example below.

Finally, remove overreaching stipulations that the customer will automatically be responsible for all fees, costs, expenses, and attorney fees related to collection. The customer should refuse to be responsible for completely unspecified and unlimited costs and fees of this kind. Consider that the amount in dispute may be $1,000, but the costs of collection $20,000. This is fundamentally unfair. Instead of stipulations of this kind, offer a mutual right for the prevailing party to recover reasonable attorney's fees in the event of a dispute.

Example Revision:

5. **Fees and Payment**

5.1 *License and Support Fees.* Customer shall pay the license, support, and other fees set forth in Exhibit A. All fees paid hereunder are non-cancellable and non-refundable (except to the extent recoverable as damages). ~~In the event of any failure to pay fees due, Customer shall reimburse Vendor for all costs of collection, including attorney's fees.~~

5.2 *Taxes.* Customer shall pay all federal, state, and local sales, use, excise, and value added taxes that are levied or imposed on the Charges~~, this Agreement, or the transactions hereunder, including sales, use, excise, and value added taxes~~ based on the license granted to Customer. In no event shall Customer be obligated to pay any tax based on the income of Vendor or its personnel. The Licensed Software and Documentation shall be delivered to Customer by electronic transmission, without delivery of physical media. The parties will reasonably cooperate in ensuring all Licensed Software and Documentation are delivered electronically in a format mutually agreed upon by the parties.

5.3 *Travel and Other Expenses.* Customer shall reimburse Vendor for all reasonable travel, living, and other out-of-pocket expenses incurred by Vendor personnel in connection with this Agreement. Notwithstanding the foregoing, Vendor shall obtain Customer's prior written approval

12 Section 5.5.

> before incurring any expenses in excess of $ ________. Customer shall not be responsible for any expenses incurred by Vendor that are not so approved.
>
> 5.4 *Payment.* Unless provided otherwise herein, Customer agrees to pay all undisputed amounts due under this Agreement within thirty (30) days of Customer's receipt of the invoice ~~after the date of invoice~~. Past due undisputed amounts will bear interest of one and one-half percent (1 1/2%) per month from the due date or the highest rate permitted by law if less. The making of any payment or payments by Customer, or the receipt thereof by Vendor, shall not imply acceptance by Customer of such items or the waiver of any warranties or requirements of this Agreement. ~~All payments made under this Agreement shall be nonrefundable, except as specifically provided otherwise in this Agreement.~~
>
> 5.5 *All Fees Stated.* Except as specifically provided in this Section 5 and in Exhibit A, there are no other fees or costs to be paid by Customer under this Agreement.

Audit Clauses

An audit clause permits the vendor to enter the licensee's place of business, review its records, and, potentially, access the licensee's computer systems to verify compliance with the license granted. Since the licensee will have possession of one of the vendor's most valued assets—its intellectual property in the form of the software—such a requirement is not generally unreasonable. Unfortunately, in recent years, these clauses have become the source of much angst between vendors and licensees. This angst arises from two sources. First, as the economy has slowed, and vendor revenue from new license deals decreased, some vendors looked to audit clauses as a way to boost revenue. Second, third-party auditors started conducting audits on a contingency basis (i.e., they would be compensated only if a discrepancy was found). The foregoing resulted in extremely invasive and disruptive audits of licensees.

To bring balance back to audit clauses, several approaches should be used. First, the number of audits the vendor may conduct should be limited to no more than once or twice in any twelve-month period during the term. Second, the scope of the audit should be limited to confirming the licensee is using the software within the scope of the license granted. Third, no third parties (other than a nationally recognized accounting firm) should be permitted access. Finally, the cost of the audit should shift only on the discovery of a truly material underpayment of fees (typically 10 percent to 20 percent) and the audit costs strictly limited to no more than a reasonable percentage of the underpayment (e.g., 25 percent).

Example Revision:

2.11 *Audit.* During the term of this Agreement and for one year thereafter, no more than once in any twelve-month period, Vendor may audit Customer's use of the Licensed Software ("Audit"). An Audit may include, without limitation, the inspection and review of computers or servers on which the Licensed Software has been installed or hosted, and records, procedures, or business practices that relate to Customer's compliance with the scope of the license granted under this ~~performance under and compliance with the terms of this~~ Agreement. Vendor or a nationally recognized accounting firm~~, its designees and agents, and any third party licensors~~ may conduct such audits. Vendor shall be responsible for ensuring any such accounting firm complies with all relevant terms of this Agreement. Before being granted access to Customer's facilities or systems, the auditor shall execute Customer's then current, generally applicable non-disclosure agreement. Vendor shall provide Customer at least thirty ~~five~~ calendar days' advance notice of an Audit. No audit will unreasonably interfere with Customer's operations. Customer will reasonably cooperate in the Audit. Under no circumstances may Vendor or its auditor directly control or access Customer's systems. All such access will be conducted by Customer personnel. The cost of the Audit shall be borne by Vendor, unless the Audit reveals an unauthorized use of the Licensed Software that results in an underpayment of license fees hereunder of more than fifteen percent (15%)~~a material breach of this Agreement by Customer (including any use of the Licensed Software in excess of the rights granted hereunder or failure to pay fees due)~~, in which case the reasonable cost of the Audit shall be paid by Customer (such cost, however, shall not exceed twenty-five percent (25%) of the underpayment in fees). In the event Customer has failed to pay all fees due, Customer shall immediately pay such fees, plus interest at the maximum rate permitted by law. If Customer has used the Licensed Software in excess of the rights granted hereunder, Customer shall pay

> all applicable additional license fees at the rates negotiated under this Agreement ~~Vendor's then current rates~~. Payment of the foregoing fees is in addition to and cumulative of all other rights of Vendor under this Agreement.

Finally, audit clauses (at least as they are commonly written) may simply not be appropriate in certain types of highly regulated industries. For example, in the financial services and health care industries, the disruptive nature of an audit and the potential for interruption of technology system performance and compromise of highly sensitive personally identifiable information has led to the use of alternatives to standard audit clauses. In those industries, the vendor is granted the right to review relevant records, but that review must occur off-site, with the vendor being granted no right to access the licensee's facilities or systems. The use of these clauses also greatly simplifies the audit process and removes the issue of third-party audit costs.

> **Example Audit Clause for Regulated Industries:**
>
> **Confirmation of Use.** No more than annually, Vendor may, upon written request to Customer, request reasonable written documentation from Customer regarding its compliance with the scope of use of the license granted hereunder. For the avoidance of doubt, Customer shall be under no obligation to (i) create or compile information that is not readily available in the ordinary course of its business; (ii) execute any scripts or other programming on its systems; or (iii) produce or disclose any personally identifiable information of a consumer. The foregoing shall not be construed as granting Vendor any right to enter Customer facilities or access Customer systems.

6. Checklist of the Key Issues

The following is a checklist of the key issues presented in this chapter:

- ☒ Definition of "Licensed Software" broadened to include all releases, versions, updates, etc.
- ☒ License grant includes all entities and personnel who will be using the software. Licensee should include allowances for anticipated future expansion of the license.

☒ The scope of the license is broad enough to encompass all intended uses of the software (e.g., not merely limited to "internal purposes").

☒ The type of license—perpetual or term—is clearly identified. A perpetual license is preferred.

☒ The list of license restrictions has been reviewed and revised to ensure the licensee may use the software for all intended purposes.

☒ All license fees and costs are clearly defined. Payments limited to undisputed amounts, with no amounts deemed non-refundable. Expenses limited to approved amounts. Taxes limited to those based on the grant of license.

☒ Software and documentation to be delivered electronically in a mutually agreed upon format.

☒ Audit provisions revised to provide balance to protect the interests of both parties.

4

Software Specifications, Acceptance Testing, and Third-Party Software

The overwhelming majority of software licenses entered into every day lack two critical elements. First, they contain no detail whatsoever from the licensee's perspective regarding the software's required functionality, interoperability, interface capabilities, etc. Apart from a vague reference to the undefined "documentation," which can change at any time, the agreement is generally silent regarding what the software will actually do for the licensee. When the vendor documentation is viewed, it is typically hyper-focused on the individual functions of each element of the software, rather than what the system as a whole will do to create value for the licensee. Second, the software—even applications licensed for millions of dollars—is not subject to any acceptance testing by the licensee. There is no procedure in the agreement permitting the licensee to test and evaluate the software to ensure the software satisfies the licensee's requirements and, worse, provides no remedy if the software fails to meet those requirements.

In addition to the lack of specifications and acceptance testing, another key area of risk is the growing use by licensors of third-party software. That is, the licensor of the primary application (i.e., the application the licensee thinks it is licensing) has embedded third-party software into the primary application. That third-party software may provide key functionality necessary for the licensee's intended use of the primary application. In many instances, including in the example agreement provided in Chapter 1, vendors are attempting to disclaim any responsibility for the third-party software they choose to include with their own software, even if the third-party software causes the primary application to malfunction and even if the third-party software causes the customer to be sued for intellectual property infringement.

In this chapter, we focus on these related issues: software specifications, acceptance testing, and third-party software. These issues are key to ensuring the licensee actually receives the full value of what it thinks it is buying.

Two brief examples will illustrate the problem.

A health care provider attended an industry conference at which it saw a demonstration of a new application being licensed by a well-known vendor. The health care provider was particularly interested in the functionality of the software relating to pharmacy management. After paying several hundred thousand dollars in license and implementation fees, the health care provider was shocked to discover that the licensor had decided not to include pharmacy functionality in its product. Because the license agreement made no reference to the pharmacy functionality and required only that the software provide the functionality in its documentation, the health care provider had no remedy under the agreement.

A large financial institution paid several million dollars to license a key piece of software. Prior to execution of the agreement, the vendor made no mention of the presence of any third-party software, and the agreement included no protections relating to third-party software. When the software was actually delivered to the customer, it included a file titled "Third Party Terms," which included nearly 200 pages of third-party agreements the customer would have to accept to use the many third-party applications incorporated into the primary application. Worse yet, the vendor assumed no responsibility for—not even an obligation to support—the third-party software it had embedded in its own application. The customer had purchased a multi-million dollar piece of software, but had no remedy if any of the many third-party applications embedded in it malfunctioned or adversely affected the operation of the primary application.

We will discuss the following sections of the form license agreement in this Chapter: Sections 1.4 (Definition of Documentation), 2.7 (Delivery), and 2.9 (Third Party Software).[13]

[13] Section 1.4, 2.7, 2.9.

Specifications and Performance Standards

The specifications are one of the most important parts—often *the* most important part—of the license agreement. Most vendor-provided agreements tie all warranties, representations, and the performance of the licensed software to the "documentation." Agreeing to this approach has several pitfalls:

- The documentation is subject to change at any time by the vendor, likely without notice to licensee. This is frequently referred to as "functionality degradation," where, over time, the functionality of the software gradually changes to exclude functionality that may have been critical to the licensee when the agreement was originally executed.
- The ability to change the documentation at any time means that the vendor can delete functionality that the licensee views as essential or change the interoperability/interface requirements of the software.
- The documentation will not include any reference to specific representations made by the vendor's sales representatives and technical staff regarding the performance of the software in the licensee's environment (both hardware and software) or its ability to meet the licensee's objectives. Instead, as noted earlier, the documentation provides technically oriented function-by-function specific directions on how to access various features of the software.

To avoid the foregoing pitfalls, the following procedure should be followed:

1. The licensee should identify any specific performance, functionality, and/or interoperability requirements for the software. These requirements should be reduced to writing and specifically identified in the body of the agreement or, more preferably, in an exhibit or other attachment. A diagram or visual of how the system is intended to work in the licensee's environment and/or plain English statement that aligns the vendor promises with the licensee's expectations can be very effective.
2. A defined term, such as "Specifications," should be added to the agreement. This term should be defined as follows: "Specifications shall mean the Licensed Software performance, functionality, and interoperability requirements set forth in this Agreement (including the

diagrams or plain English statements referred to above) and, to the extent not inconsistent with the foregoing, the Documentation."[14]

3. All warranties and other performance representations that originally required compliance with the Vendor's "documentation" should be revised to require compliance with the newly defined "Specifications."
4. Acceptance and testing provisions should be revised to require compliance with the Specifications as a condition to passing the test and acceptance.
5. Expand the vendor's definition of documentation to include all materials the vendor has provided to the licensee relating to the software, including training manuals, online help files, technical information, etc.

Even if there are no specifications in a particular engagement, and the licensee is willing to assume the risk of having functionality "float" with the vendor's documentation, it should consider including a firewall to prevent functionality from materially diminishing during the term of the agreement. For example, where the agreement refers to the vendor's "then current Documentation," insert a qualification such as "any modification to the Documentation will not reflect an overall material decrease in the functionality or performance of the Licensed Software from that existing on the Effective Date."

The most important point to take away from this discussion is that a prudent licensee should not rely on the vendor's documentation to ensure the licensed software will perform as the licensee requires. Rather, the licensee should take the time to identify the elements of the software that are critical to achieving its goals in licensing the application and to specifically incorporate those elements into the agreement.

Example Revision:

1.4 "Documentation" shall mean <u>Vendor's training course materials, system specifications, hardware requirements, technical manuals, and all other user instructions regarding the capabilities, operation, installation, and</u>

---

[14] If the licensee has prepared a Request For Proposals and the vendor has provided a Response to the Request for Proposals, those documents should be included in the definition of "Specifications": "Specifications shall mean the Licensed Software performance and interoperability requirements set forth in this Agreement, licensee's Request for Proposals, Vendor's Response to the Request for Proposals, and, to the extent not inconsistent with the foregoing, the Documentation."

> use of the Licensed Software, including all online help files and other user instructions ~~Vendor's then current documentation for the Licensed Software~~. Any modification to the Documentation will not reflect an overall material decrease in the functionality or performance of the Licensed Software from that existing on the Effective Date.
>
> 1.5[15] "Specifications" shall mean the requirements set forth in this Agreement, Exhibit A (Required Functionality),[16] and, solely to the extent not inconsistent with the foregoing, the Documentation.

Acceptance Testing

The vast majority of vendor agreements provide for no acceptance testing of the software being licensed. If the issue is addressed at all, the agreement generally provides that the software will be automatically "deemed accepted" after some period of time, usually thirty or sixty days from delivery. In the vendor form agreement in Chapter 1, Section 2.7[17] provides that the Licensed Software is deemed accepted on delivery. This type of automatic acceptance should be strictly avoided because it could easily result in the licensee paying for a product that does not work or interface correctly.

Acceptance (and payment) should not occur until the licensee has satisfied itself that the software is performing in accordance with the agreed upon specifications. A good practice is to withhold 20 percent to 25 percent of the license fees until after final acceptance. This will ensure vendor's "interest" throughout the testing process. Where appropriate, the agreement should also provide for interim testing of deliverables (e.g., at defined steps in the implementation process). This will help identify potential problems or deficiencies early in the process, rather than at the end. For example, testing could be conducted in stages as follows:

1. *Installation testing*: Performed on delivery of the software to confirm basic functionality and performance.
2. *Interface testing*: Testing of each interface as it is implemented.
3. *Component/module testing*: Testing of each component or module of the software as it is implemented (e.g., in an accounting package, the

[15] Proposed new section defining "Specifications" for the Licensed Software.

[16] In this agreement, the licensee has attached an Exhibit A that lists all of the critical functionality for the software.

[17] Section 2.7.

licensee would test the accounts payable module, accounts receivable module, etc.).

4. *Final system testing.* Testing of all components and modules of the software working on the licensee's systems, with all interfaces implemented.

The agreement should be revised to include a specific acceptance testing provision that includes the procedures to be followed if the software fails the applicable acceptance test. If, after several attempts, the vendor is unable to provide software that conforms to the specifications, the licensee should have the right to terminate the license and receive a refund of all fees paid, including all license, support, and professional service fees. Some vendors may balk at a full refund of all fees paid, but they must be forced to assume responsibility for failing to provide what they agreed in writing to deliver. If a vendor licenses an application and charges the licensee $50,000 to install it, and the application fails to work, the vendor should not be allowed to keep the professional service fees. To agree otherwise would remove a substantial incentive for the vendor to make sure the software works as agreed upon in the license agreement.

Vendors will aggressively resist efforts to tie acceptance to payment, frequently citing revenue recognition issues. While it is true that there are standards governing how vendors can report revenue for software sales in the face of contingencies surrounding payment, this issue should not immunize the vendor from deferring some portion of payment until it has delivered a software product that is functioning as the parties agreed.

Example Revision:

2.7 *Delivery.* Vendor will deliver the object code version of the Licensed Software to Customer within five (5) days of the Reference Date. Vendor will bear risk of loss of the Licensed Software until delivered at the Customer designated facility. ~~Customer will be deemed to have accepted the Licensed Software on delivery.~~

2.8[18] *Acceptance Testing.* Customer shall have sixty (60) days from the date of delivery to test the Licensed Software to determine whether it complies in all material respects with the Specifications. Upon completion of the

[18] Proposed new section providing acceptance testing procedures.

> testing, Customer shall promptly notify Vendor whether it has accepted the Licensed Software ("Accept") or whether it has identified discrepancies with the Specifications ("Reject"). If Customer Rejects the Licensed Software, Customer shall provide a written list of items that must be corrected. On receipt of Customer's notice, Vendor shall promptly commence, at no additional charge to Customer, all reasonable efforts to complete, as quickly as possible, such necessary corrections, repairs, and modifications to the Licensed Software as will permit it to be ready for retesting and review, but in no event shall such corrective measures exceed twenty (20) days from receipt of Customer's notice. The testing and evaluation process shall resume, as set forth above. If Customer Accepts the Licensed Software, it shall issue a written "Acceptance Notice." The date of such Acceptance Notice shall be deemed the "Acceptance Date." If Customer determines the Licensed Software, as revised, still does not comply in all material respects with the Specifications, Customer may either (1) afford Vendor the opportunity to repeat the correction and modification process as set forth above at no additional cost or charge to Customer, or (2) depending on the nature and extent of the failure in Customer's sole judgment, terminate this Agreement. The foregoing correction and modification procedure shall be repeated until the Licensed Software is Accepted or Customer elects to terminate the Agreement as provided above. In the event of a termination under this Section, Vendor shall pay to Customer, within ten (10) business days of written notice of termination, all sums paid to Vendor by Customer under this Agreement for the Licensed Software, including all professional service fees and prepaid support fees.

Some vendors may accept the suggested language shown in Section 2.8, above, but want to include the concept that if the customer fails to reject or otherwise respond during the acceptance period, the software will be "deemed accepted." The vendor is reasonably concerned with ensuring that the customer will not later circle back with a complaint after the acceptance period has run out and is concerned that any fees payable on acceptance become due and payable.

Customers should continue to strive to avoid "deemed" accepted language because it may imply the software is actually conforming. They can, however, make clear that if they fail to respond within the acceptance period, they cannot later reject the software under the acceptance provision, and any fees payable on acceptance would become due. If the vendor insists on stating the software is deemed accepted, the customer should insert a parenthetical or other qualification making clear this does not mean the vendor is being relieved of any of its other obligations under the agreement, and, in particular, deemed acceptance does not result in a waiver of the vendor's warranty obligations.

Third-Party Software

Third party software can take one of two forms:

Open source software: The third-party software may constitute open source software—software that has been written by potentially dozens or even hundreds of developers all over the world, made available on an as-is basis in source code form and without charge from various sites on the Internet. For most open source software, it is impossible to determine whether the various developers had sufficient intellectual property rights to contribute their code to the software.

Proprietary software: The other type of third-party software is software developed and licensed by third parties under commercial licenses for a fee. This proprietary software is generally provided in object code form only and may come with various warranties and other protections.

If a vendor elects to include either type of third-party software in its application, the vendor should be expected to stand behind the third-party software (through warranties, intellectual property indemnification, support, ensuring ongoing compatibility, etc.). If, on the other hand, the vendor is permitted to disclaim all responsibility for that software, as is the case in Section 2.9 of the vendor agreement shown in Chapter 1, the value of the software the customer is purchasing could be greatly undermined. The customer would have no remedy if the third-party software contained a bug or virus, was incompatible with the other software, or became the subject of an intellectual property infringement claim. Worse yet, even if a failure in the third-party software rendered the primary application being licensed entirely unusable, the customer might be forced to continue to pay for the useless software, without any means of declaring a breach of the license agreement.

In addition to the risks outlined above, the presence of third-party software almost always means the customer must accept and be bound by various third-party license agreements—agreements (pass-through provisions) that the customer may not even see until after execution of its license agreement and that can change at any time.

Always make sure to review and assess all third-party software license agreements to identify any problematic terms. In particular, be mindful of any limits on the scope of the license that might impact the customer's ability to fully use the primary software it is licensing. The pass-through provisions may also narrow protections from the vendor that the customer thought were secured by the license agreement for the primary application. Do not treat the pass-through provisions as an inconsequential or non-negotiable element of the transaction.

To mitigate the risks of third-party software, the license agreement should include language requiring the vendor to clearly identify the presence of the software, provide copies of the relevant third-party license agreements, and assume responsibility for the third-party software.

Example Third Party Software Provision:

2.9 ***Third-Party Software.*** In the event Vendor provides any third-party software (the "Third-Party Software"), including Open Source Software, to Customer in connection with this Agreement for which Customer would be obligated to accept and be bound by any third-party terms and conditions, the following shall apply: (1) Vendor shall specifically identify in writing all Third-Party Software in the relevant Order Document; (2) Vendor shall attach to the relevant Order Document written copies of all third-party license agreements applicable to Customer; and (3) Vendor warrants that (i) it has the right to license any Third-Party Software licensed to Customer under this Agreement; (ii) to the best of Vendor's knowledge, the Third-Party Software does not, and the use of the Third-Party Software by Customer as contemplated by this Agreement will not, infringe any intellectual property rights of any third party; and (iii) unless specifically provided otherwise herein, Customer shall have no obligation to pay any third party any fees, royalties, or other payments for Customer's use of any Third-Party Software in accordance with the terms of this Agreement.

> With regard to (i) Open Source Software, (ii) any Third-Party Software that Vendor fails to identify in the relevant Order Document, and (iii) any third-party software embedded in the Licensed Software for which Customer is not required to accept any third-party terms and conditions, all such software shall be considered, as appropriate, part of and included in the definition of "Licensed Software" and subject to all warranties, indemnities, and other requirements of this Agreement, including scope of license and maintenance and support, relating to the Licensed Software. To the extent permitted by law or contract, Vendor shall pass through to Customer the warranties for the Third-Party Software. For purposes of this provision, "Open Source Software" means any software, programming, or other intellectual property that is subject to (i) the GNU General Public License, GNU Library General Public License, Artistic License, BSD license, Mozilla Public License, or any similar license, including, but not limited to, those licenses listed at www.opensource.org/licenses or (ii) any agreement with terms requiring any intellectual property owned or licensed by Customer to be (a) disclosed or distributed in source code or object code form; (b) licensed for the purpose of making derivative works; or (c) redistributable.

4. Checklist of Key Issues

The following is a checklist of the key issues presented in this chapter:

- ☒ Make sure the vendor's definition of "documentation" includes all possible documents, information, and other materials relating to the software being licensed.
- ☒ If the licensee has specific performance, functionality and/or interoperability requirements for the software, those requirements should be incorporated into the agreement. The licensee should not rely on vendor representations that the software will simply do what is in the documentation. Use of diagrams to show or plain English statements to describe what the software is expected to do from the customer's perspective is highly recommended.
- ☒ Reject all language relating to automatic acceptance of applications.
- ☒ Except in limited circumstances (e.g., off-the-shelf software, software with which the licensee is already experienced), all software should be subject to acceptance testing. The acceptance testing provision in the

license agreement should provide a specific procedure for testing, acceptance, and rejection. If the software fails acceptance testing, the licensee should receive a full refund of all fees paid.

☒ Always hold back a portion of the license fees until acceptance is achieved.

☒ Require the vendor to identify all third-party software and applicable license agreements and to assume responsibility for the performance of that software. Make sure to review all third-party licenses to identify any problematic terms.

5

Warranties, Indemnities, and Limitation of Liability

Three of the most difficult areas of negotiation in licensing transactions are the vendor's warranties, indemnities, and limitation of liability. The approach used in most vendor form agreements is to warrant little, provide a narrow indemnity for intellectual property infringement, and limit the vendor's liability to, at best, a fraction of the fees paid under the agreement. While it is not generally possible or reasonable to require a vendor to assume unlimited liability for the performance of its software, it is possible, by standing firm on these issues, to dramatically improve the protections typically offered by vendors in this area.

As noted in the Forward to this second edition, one of the most alarming trends in software licensing is that some vendors are now declining even basic responsibility in their customer agreements. Even in contracts involving substantial fees, some vendors take the position that their software is essentially provided as-is, that they will assume little responsibility for intellectual property infringement claims they cause, and, at the end of the day, that they limit their liability to a trivial amount. The agreements are so one-sided that even if the vendor intentionally fails to perform, the customer has little or no remedy—other than to forfeit its entire investment. Customers should reject this approach of shifting the entire risk of a software licensing engagement onto themselves. They should insist on a reasonable balance of risk.

This chapter discusses the protections licensees can reasonably expect to negotiate and should insist on in most licensing transactions. Moving vendors on these issues is not easy. Customers must raise these issues at the outset and be resolved to potential ongoing vendor pushback. Unless achieving a fair balance of risk is demonstrated as critical to the customer, and not just a legal issue, it is unlikely the customer will achieve meaningful vendor movement on these issues.

The following sections of the form license agreement are discussed in this Chapter: 7 (Limited Warranties), 8 (Disclaimer of Warranties), 9 (Limitation of Liability), and 11 (Indemnity).

Warranties

It is common for vendors to exclude nearly every type of warranty, including the implied warranties of merchantability and fitness of the product for licensee's intended uses. This is neither fair nor appropriate. At minimum, the vendor should be required to provide the following basic warranties:

- *Performance.* That the software will perform in accordance with agreed-upon product Specifications[19] and that the warranty period should extend for at least twelve, if not twenty-four, months from the date of acceptance[20] (not delivery). In most instances, the preferred approach is to have the warranty period extend for the entire time during which the licensee purchases support services from the vendor.
- *Services.* That the vendor's services (e.g., installation, implementation, and support services) will be provided in a timely, workmanlike manner, in compliance with industry best practices.
- *Compliance with applicable law.* That the software will comply with all federal, state, and local laws, rules, and regulations. Licensees in certain industries may require specific warranties relating to issues that are unique to their businesses. For example, a broker/dealer may require a warranty that the licensor will comply with privacy requirements of the Gramm-Leach Bliley Act (GLB) and its implementing regulations. Similarly, a health care provider may require a warranty that the licensor will comply with the privacy requirements of the Health Insurance Portability and Accountability Act (HIPAA).

---

[19] *See* discussion of "Specifications" in Chapter 4.
[20] *See* discussion of acceptance testing in Chapter 4.

- *Infringement of intellectual property.* That the software will not infringe the intellectual property rights of any third person. Astute vendors will generally refuse such a blanket warranty. In such cases, the warranty can be limited to a representation by the vendor that, to the best of its knowledge, the software does not infringe the intellectual property rights of any third person. Such a knowledge-based warranty, in combination with an indemnity obligation for infringement claims,[21] generally provides sufficient protection for the licensee.
- *Viruses.* That the software will be free from viruses and other destructive programs.
- *Disabling mechanisms.* That the software does not contain any time bomb or lock-up mechanisms. When triggered by the vendor, these mechanisms can cause the software and the licensee's data to become unusable and inaccessible. Vendors may use these protections to disable the software after the term of the license, but, more frequently, they use them to gain an unfair advantage in the event of a dispute during the term. For example, if the parties are involved in a dispute over professional service fees, the vendor could trigger the disabling mechanism to shut the software down until the dispute is resolved. The use of these "self-help" mechanisms is inappropriate in all but a very narrow range of applications (e.g., a piece of off-the-shelf software licensed for a defined trial period after which the software will not be useable until the licensee purchases a term or perpetual license). Because they could literally bring the licensee's business to a halt, specific contractual provisions should be included in the license agreement prohibiting their use. Although the substance of this warranty is important, it is equally important to discuss the subject with the licensor to determine whether it routinely utilizes disabling devices in its software.
- *Third-party software.* That the licensor has specifically identified in an exhibit to the agreement all third-party software to be delivered by the licensor to the licensee in connection with the licensed software.[22] In many instances, the licensor may have incorporated software from various third parties into its product. The third-party licensors may require the licensee to be bound to their own terms

[21] *See* discussion of indemnity protections in this Chapter.

[22] *See* Chapter 4 for a further discussion of third-party software.

and conditions and potentially to pay separate license fees for the use of their software. One leading vendor makes no mention in its form license agreement that it will be delivering literally dozens of third-party applications with its software. Each application requires the licensee to accept a different set of third-party terms and conditions. The presence of these third-party applications is not disclosed to the licensee until the agreement has been signed and the software delivered. To avoid such surprises, the licensor should be under an affirmative obligation to identify specifically each item of third-party software in an exhibit to the license agreement.

- *Authority.* That the licensor has sufficient authority to enter into the license agreement and grant the rights provided in the agreement to the licensee.
- *Litigation.* That there is no pending litigation involving the vendor that may impair or interfere with the licensee's right to use the product.

Four additional points should be kept in mind when reviewing warranty provisions in license agreements.

First, beware of very general disclaimer language that could undermine or potentially conflict with express warranties provided elsewhere in the agreement. It is not uncommon to find vendor form agreements with one or two express warranties and then find a general disclaimer provision that states the software is "provided without warranties of any kind" or that the software is "provided as-is." These types of general disclaimers directly conflict with any express warranties provided in the agreement and should be specifically qualified as shown in the example revision to our vendor form agreement below.

The second issue to bear in mind is the growing trend by many vendors to incorporate third-party software, particularly open source software, into their applications. This is done to expedite development time and reduce cost and for other considerations. In addition to the warranty described above regarding third-party applications, the licensee should consider including language in the agreement requiring the licensor to assign or "pass through" to the licensee any warranties the licensor received from those third parties. Specifically, the licensor will have entered into license agreements with each of the third-party licensors. Those license agreements may, and likely will, contain warranties that can be passed through to the licensee. For example, "To the extent permissible, Licensor hereby assigns to Customer any warranties made to Licensor by any Third-Party Licensors." This is a no-cost act by the licensor, but is a valuable asset to the licensee.

The third issue is the avoidance of exclusive remedies. Most vendor form agreements include language similar to the following: "In the event of a breach of warranty, Customer's sole and exclusive remedy and Vendor's sole and exclusive liability shall be for Vendor to use reasonable efforts to repair the defective software." There are a number of problems presented by this approach. Foremost among them is that there is no time limit within which the repair must be made. If a critical defect exists in the software that renders it unusable, this language places no limit on the length of time the licensor can take to identify and repair the defect. It may take a week. It may take six months. In the meantime, the licensee is left with a piece of software it cannot use. The preferred approach to such provisions is to delete them in their entirety. The licensee should have whatever rights are available to it under the agreement in the event the licensor breaches a warranty. If the provision cannot be deleted, it should be strictly qualified to require the licensor to provide a remedy within a defined period (e.g., thirty days).

Finally, the scope of the warranties should be carefully reviewed to ensure they cover all aspects of the software being licensed and services to be performed. Consider the warranty provided in Section 7.1 of the vendor form agreement. This warranty is limited to the "Licensed Software." As discussed in Chapter 3, the definition of this term must be revised to ensure it includes future releases and versions of the software. All defined terms in vendor-provided warranties should be reviewed for similar discrepancies.

Example Revision:

7. **Limited Warranty**

7.1 *Licensed Software.* Vendor warrants that the Licensed Software shall perform substantially in accordance with the requirements of this Agreement and, solely to the extent not inconsistent, the documentation for the greater of (i) ~~a period of~~ one (1) year ~~ninety (90) days~~ after the date of Acceptance ~~Reference Date~~ or (ii) the period during which Customer purchases support from Vendor (the "~~Initial~~ Warranty Period"). Customer shall provide written notice of any warranty failure to Vendor not less than five (5) days prior to the end of the ~~Initial~~ Warranty Period. Such notice shall specify with particularity the nature of any such failure. Vendor shall not be responsible for any errors or nonconformities in the Licensed Software resulting from Customer's ~~misuse, negligence,~~ failure to use the Licensed Software in conformance with this Agreement or modification of the Licensed Software by Customer.

7.2 *Services.* Vendor warrants that all services provided by Vendor to Customer under this Agreement shall be performed in a workmanlike manner.

7.3[23] *Viruses and Disabling Mechanisms.* Vendor shall use commercially reasonable measures to screen the Licensed Software to avoid introducing any virus or other destructive programming that are designed (i) to permit unauthorized access or use by third parties to the software installed on Customer's systems, or (ii) to disable or damage Customer's systems. Vendor shall not insert into the Licensed Software any code or other device that would have the effect of disabling or otherwise shutting down all or any portion of the Licensed Software. Vendor shall not invoke such code or other device at any time, including upon expiration or termination of this Agreement for any reason.

7.4 *Infringement.* To the best of Vendor's knowledge, Customer's permitted use of the Licensed Software will not infringe the intellectual property rights of any third party.

7.5 *No Litigation.* Vendor further warrants there is no pending or threatened litigation that would have a material adverse impact on its performance under this Agreement.

7.6 *Authority.* Vendor has the full power, capacity, and authority to enter into and perform this Agreement and to make the grant of rights contained herein.

7.7 *Compliance with Applicable Law.* Vendor warrants that the services provided under this Agreement and Customer's permitted use of the Licensed Software shall comply with applicable federal, state, and local laws and regulations.

7.8 *Third-Party Software.* In the event Vendor provides any third-party software (the "Third-Party Software") to Customer in connection with this Agreement, the following shall apply: (1) Vendor shall specifically identify in

---

[23] Sections 7.3 through 7.8 are example additional warranties that may be added to vendor form license agreements.

writing all Third-Party Software in Exhibit __; (2) Vendor shall attach to Exhibit __ written copies of all third-party license agreements applicable to Customer; and (3) Vendor warrants that (i) it has the right to license any Third-Party Software licensed to Customer under this Agreement; (ii) to the best of Vendor's knowledge, the Third-Party Software does not, and the use of the Third Party Software by Customer as contemplated by this Agreement, will not, infringe any intellectual property rights of any third party; and (iii) unless specifically provided otherwise herein, Customer shall have no obligation to pay any third party any fees, royalties, or other payments for Customer's use of any Third-Party Software in accordance with the terms of this Agreement. Vendor shall support and maintain all such Third-Party Software to the same extent as the Licensed Software.

8. **Disclaimer of Warranties**

<u>EXCEPT AS PROVIDED IN SECTION 7</u>, VENDOR EXPRESSLY DISCLAIMS ALL <u>OTHER</u> WARRANTIES, EXPRESS AND IMPLIED, INCLUDING, BUT NOT LIMITED TO, THE IMPLIED WARRANTIES OF MERCHANTABILITY AND FITNESS FOR A PARTICULAR PURPOSE. VENDOR DOES NOT WARRANT THAT THE PRODUCTS WILL MEET CUSTOMER'S REQUIREMENTS, THAT THE LICENSED SOFTWARE IS COMPATIBLE WITH ANY PARTICULAR HARDWARE OR SOFTWARE PLATFORM, OR THAT THE OPERATION OF THE LICENSED SOFTWARE WILL BE UNINTERRUPTED OR ERROR-FREE, OR THAT DEFECTS IN THE LICENSED SOFTWARE WILL BE CORRECTED. THE ENTIRE RISK AS TO THE RESULTS AND PERFORMANCE OF THE LICENSED SOFTWARE IS ASSUMED BY CUSTOMER. FURTHERMORE, <u>EXCEPT AS PROVIDED IN SECTION 7</u>, VENDOR DOES NOT WARRANT OR MAKE ANY REPRESENTATION REGARDING THE USE OR THE RESULTS OF THE USE OF THE LICENSED SOFTWARE OR RELATED DOCUMENTATION IN TERMS OF THEIR CORRECTNESS, ACCURACY, QUALITY, RELIABILITY, APPROPRIATENESS FOR A PARTICULAR TASK OR APPLICATION, CURRENTNESS, OR OTHERWISE. NO ORAL OR WRITTEN INFORMATION OR ADVICE GIVEN BY VENDOR OR VENDOR'S AUTHORIZED REPRESENTATIVES SHALL CREATE A WARRANTY OR IN ANY WAY INCREASE THE SCOPE OF WARRANTIES PROVIDED IN THIS AGREEMENT.

Licensor Indemnity Obligations

Under a contractual indemnity provision, one party (the indemnitor) agrees to protect another party (the indemnitee) from claims by third parties arising out of the indemnitor's conduct. The most common example of this type of provision is the indemnity provided by most vendors to protect their licensees from claims that the licensed software infringes the intellectual property rights of a third party. If the third party sues the licensee claiming the licensee's use of the software infringes its intellectual property rights, the vendor will hire a lawyer to defend the licensee and pay any damages that result from the claim.

Intellectual Property Infringement Indemnity

The intellectual property rights indemnity protects against events that do not occur with great frequency. However, it is somewhat like earthquake insurance in that, if there is an infringement claim, the potential costs to the licensee would be significant, and the licensee's continued use of the software could be precluded. Consequently, the indemnity provision is extremely important, and despite vendor protestations that they have never had an infringement claim or ever heard of such a claim, this protection should be required from all licensors. This protection has gained even more importance recently as the number of intellectual property infringement actions is on the rise, particularly those relating to patent infringement.

Vendors often try to limit the intellectual property indemnification to infringement of copyrights only. That is not acceptable, as most infringement actions arise out of patent or trade secret rights. The indemnity should extend to infringement claims of any "patent, copyright, trade secret, or other proprietary rights of a third party." The vendor may also try to limit the indemnification to "United States" intellectual property rights, and unless foreign use of the software is anticipated, this limitation is generally acceptable.

Some vendors may insist on certain exceptions to their indemnity obligation. Common and acceptable exception language is as follows:

> Notwithstanding anything to the contrary herein, Vendor shall not be responsible under this Section for infringement

> claims arising from (i) modifications of the Licensed Software by any party other than Vendor or its agents; (ii) specifications provided by Customer for the development of custom programming; and (iii) failure to implement an update to the Licensed Software that would have avoided the infringement.

With regard to the last exception, it is important to include the following qualifying language: "(iii) failure to implement an update to the Licensed Software that would have avoided the infringement, provided Vendor has notified Customer in writing that use of the update would have avoided the claim."

Most recently, vendors have started to include exceptions to their indemnity obligations for patent claims by "non-practicing entities," which refers to so-called patent trolls.[24] Since patent trolls are in many cases the most likely entity to sue for infringement, excluding this category of claim greatly dilutes the customer's protections.

If the licensee's use of the product is prevented by court order, or if the business risks (potential exposure to punitive damages) of continued use of the product are too great for the licensee, the licensee must have the option to demand that the vendor (i) procure the rights for continued use of the product by licensee, (ii) replace or modify the product with another system or components of comparable quality and functionality, or (iii) refund all fees, including license and professional service fees, paid by the licensee.[25] Many licenses give the vendor the right to choose the remedies described in Sections (i) through (iii). These provisions should be modified to give the option to the licensee, or at a minimum, require the vendor to use commercially reasonable efforts to accomplish (i) or (ii) before resorting to (iii). One of the most common errors in drafting these types of provisions is the failure to include a specific period for the vendor to provide one of the remedies described above. *See* the example language provided below.

---

[24] A non-practicing entity (NPE), or patent troll, is generally defined as a person or entity that accumulates a large patent portfolio for the purpose of deriving revenue not from putting them into useful practice in products or services, but from enforcing the patent rights against third parties.

[25] Depending on the size of the transaction and bargaining strength of the licensee, the licensee should consider requiring the vendor (in addition to refunding the purchase, license, and professional service fees paid for the product) also to reimburse the licensee for all reasonable costs incurred by the licensee associated with having to seek, negotiate, and switch to another vendor.

Other Vendor Indemnities

In addition to an indemnity for intellectual property infringement, the unique circumstances of a particular transaction may cause the licensee to request other indemnities from the vendor. If the licensee is a health care provider or a financial institution, and the vendor will have access to non-public patient or customer information in implementing the software, the licensee may require the vendor to indemnify the licensee from any claims arising from the vendor's breach of confidentiality with regard to the patient or customer information. Other common indemnities include the following:

- *Property damage.* Indemnity from claims arising from damage or destruction of property caused by the vendor.
- *Personal injury.* Indemnity from claims arising from personal injury claims resulting from the actions of the vendor and its employees.
- *Employee compensation claims.* Since the vendor is an independent contractor of the licensee, the licensee should have no liability for compensation, overtime, and other similar claims by the licensor's employees. This indemnity requires the licensor to indemnify the licensee from those claims.

Licensee Indemnities

Vendors frequently seek very broad indemnities from their licensees regarding use of their software. The indemnity in Section 10 of the vendor form agreement shows a typical licensee indemnification provision. Note that unlike the vendor indemnities described above, there is no "fault" component in this provision. Specifically, the common thread running through the vendor indemnities described above is that the licensee is being protected from claims that arise because of some fault of the vendor (e.g., the vendor has infringed a third party's intellectual property rights; the vendor has damaged a third party's property; the vendor has injured someone). Compare the indemnity in Section 10 of the form agreement. This provision requires the licensee to protect the vendor from claims—*even if the licensee has done nothing wrong, even if the claim arises because of something the vendor has done.* This provision requires the licensee to indemnify the vendor for any claims that may arise from the licensed software, regardless of whether the licensee is at fault.

Consider the following examples. A third party sues the licensee and the vendor because the vendor intentionally infringed the third party's intellectual property rights. In that case, Section 10 would require the licensee to hire a lawyer to defend the vendor from its own wrongful conduct and to pay any damages a court may award. Similarly, if a defect in the software causes a third party harm, the licensee must indemnify the vendor from any claims by that third party.

Licensee indemnities that are not based on fault are unfair and unreasonable and should be strongly resisted. At most, the licensee should indemnify the vendor from the following types of claims:

1. Intellectual property provided by the licensee that infringes a third party's intellectual property rights (the reciprocal of the standard vendor intellectual property infringement indemnity)
2. Licensee's failure to use the software as permitted under the agreement
3. Licensee's modification of the vendor's software, solely to the extent the infringement claim results from those modifications

Example Revision:

10. **Indemnification**[26]

10.1 *Customer Indemnification.* Customer shall defend, indemnify, and hold Vendor and its directors, officers, agents, employees, members, subsidiaries, and affiliates from and against any claim, action, proceeding, liability, loss, damage, cost, or expense (including, without limitation, attorneys' fees), arising out of or in connection with Customer's failure to use ~~of~~ the Licensed Software as permitted under this Agreement. Vendor shall provide Customer with prompt notice of any such claims, allow the Customer sole control of the defense, and fully cooperate with the Customer in defending the claim.

10.2 *Vendor Indemnification.*[27] Vendor, at its own expense (including payment of attorneys' fees, expert fees, and court costs) shall defend Customer and its directors, officers, agents, employees, subsidiaries, and successors in interest

[26] Note that we have split the existing indemnification section into two parts: Customer Indemnification and Vendor Indemnification.

[27] Proposed new section providing a standard vendor indemnity for intellectual property infringement.

> against any loss, cost, damage, liability, or expense from any and all third-party claims that the License Software infringes any patent, copyright, trade secret, or other proprietary right of a third party and shall indemnify and hold harmless Customer and its directors, officers, agents, employees, subsidiaries, and successors in interest from any amounts assessed against them in a resulting judgment or amounts to settle such claims, provided that Customer (a) gives Vendor prompt written notice of any such claim, (b) permits Vendor to control and direct the defense or settlement of any such claim, and (c) provides Vendor all reasonable assistance (at the expense of Vendor) in connection with the defense or settlement of any such claim. If the Licensed Software is, or is likely to be, the subject of an infringement claim, Vendor, at its expense, shall: (i) procure the right to allow Customer to continue to use the Licensed Software; or (ii) modify or replace the Licensed Software or infringing portions thereof to become non-infringing, without loss of material functionality. If Vendor is unable to provide one of the remedies in (i) or (ii) within forty-five (45) days of notice of the claim (unless such period is extended by Customer), Vendor shall have the right to terminate this Agreement and refund all fees paid hereunder for the Licensed Software, pro-rated on a straight-line basis over a five-year term. Notwithstanding the foregoing, Vendor shall have no obligations under this Section solely to the extent any infringement claim is based upon or arising out of (i) any modification or alteration to the Licensed Software not approved by Vendor, (ii) any combination or use of the Licensed Software with products or services not supplied by Vendor or approved in writing by Vendor in advance of such combination, or (iii) use of the Licensed Software not in accordance with the applicable Documentation or outside the scope of the license granted under this Agreement.

Limitation of Liability

There are two general categories of damages recoverable for breach of a license agreement: consequential damages and direct damages. Consequential damages include lost profits, damage to data, data recovery costs, consulting fees, and damage to business reputation, etc. Consequential damages are sometimes called "incidental," "indirect," or "special" damages. Direct or "actual" damages are directly referable to breach of the agreement. For example, if software fails to perform, direct damages would be the license fee paid for the software, while consequential damages would include the lost profits that result from the licensee's inability to use the software. Almost all commercial software licenses have "limitation of liability" provisions that specifically disclaim liability for consequential damages and typically limit direct damages to all or some portion of the fees paid for the software. While it is not generally possible to eliminate the limitation of liability in its entirety, the following concessions can usually be obtained:

- The limitation of liability should be made applicable to *both* parties. The licensee should be entitled to essentially the same protections from damages that the vendor is seeking.
- The following should be excluded from *all* limitations of liability and damages:
    - Breach of the confidentiality provision by either party;
    - Claims for which vendor is insured; and
    - The parties' respective indemnity obligations (particularly for intellectual property infringement).
- The overall liability cap (usually limited to fees paid) should be increased to some multiple of *all* license and professional service fees paid (e.g., one and one-half to three times the total fees). The licensee should bear in mind that the overall liability cap must not apply to the exclusions set forth in the bullet point above.

From the licensee's standpoint, it is optimal for the agreement to be silent on the issue of limitations of liability and damages. If the agreement is silent, then each party is responsible for all damages that they are determined to have caused. That position should be acceptable to the licensee because the licensee's only real obligation under the agreement is payment. Unfortunately, virtually every licensor-drafted agreement contains an extremely expansive limitation of liability provision that often limits the licensor's liability to a fraction of the amount that it has been paid. This is neither fair nor appropriate, and the licensee must strenuously object to any broad form of limitations.

As shown in the example revision below, it is important to draft that the overall liability cap is appropriate in the early days of the agreement, when potentially only a small amount in fees will have been paid. If the cap is framed in terms of "all fees paid," and the amount of those fees early in the agreement is small, the licensee will have little real protection if the vendor breaches. One approach to address this problem is to draft the liability cap in terms of the greater of fees paid or some defined amount (typically set at the fees to be paid during the first six months to twelve months of the agreement).

One of the most common errors made by licensees in negotiating limitation of liability provisions is the failure to ensure that any exceptions from the limitation (indemnity obligations, breach of confidentiality, insured claims, etc.) are carved out of *both* the exclusion of consequential damages and the overall liability cap. Most limitation of liability provisions (as shown in Section 9 of the vendor form license) are divided into two parts: the exclusion of consequential damages and the overall liability cap. These two parts are generally set forth in two separate sentences within the limitation of liability clause. It is critical that the exceptions be carved out of both *sentences*. This is shown in the example revision below.

Example Revision:

9. ***Limitation of Liability***. EXCEPT FOR BREACH OF SECTION 6 (CONFIDENTIALITY), INSURED CLAIMS, AND THE PARTIES' RESPECTIVE EXPRESS INDEMNITY OBLIGATIONS, IN NO EVENT SHALL EITHER PARTY ~~VENDOR~~ BE LIABLE TO THE OTHER PARTY~~CUSTOMER~~ OR ANY THIRD PARTY FOR ANY INCIDENTAL OR CONSEQUENTIAL DAMAGES (INCLUDING, WITHOUT LIMITATION, INDIRECT, SPECIAL, PUNITIVE, OR EXEMPLARY DAMAGES FOR LOSS OF BUSINESS, LOSS OF PROFITS, BUSINESS INTERRUPTION, LOSS OF DATA, OR LOSS OF BUSINESS INFORMATION) ARISING OUT OF THIS AGREEMENT OR CONNECTED IN ANY WAY WITH USE OF OR INABILITY TO USE THE LICENSED SOFTWARE, OR FOR ANY CLAIM BY ANY OTHER PARTY, EVEN IF THE PARTY ~~VENDOR~~ HAS BEEN ADVISED OF THE POSSIBILITY OF SUCH DAMAGES. EXCEPT FOR BREACH OF SECTION 6 (CONFIDENTIALITY), INSURED CLAIMS, AND THE PARTIES' RESPECTIVE EXPRESS INDEMNITY OBLIGATIONS, THE ~~VENDOR'S~~ TOTAL LIABILITY OF EITHER PARTY TO THE OTHER PARTY ~~TO CUSTOMER~~ FOR ALL DAMAGES, LOSSES, AND CAUSES OF ACTION (WHETHER IN CONTRACT, TORT (INCLUDING NEGLIGENCE), OR

OTHERWISE) SHALL NOT EXCEED THE GREATER OF (I) TWO TIMES THE AGGREGATE FEES PAID HEREUNDER~~PURCHASE PRICE~~ OR (II) $100,000. THE LIMITATIONS PROVIDED IN THIS SECTION SHALL APPLY EVEN IF ANY OTHER REMEDIES FAIL OF THEIR ESSENTIAL PURPOSE.

Checklist of Key Issues

The following is a checklist of the key issues presented in this chapter:

- ☒ Negotiate basic warranty protections: (1) performance, (2) services, (3) compliance with applicable law, (4) intellectual property infringement, (5) freedom from viruses, (6) no disabling mechanisms, (7) third-party software, (8) authority, and (9) no pending or threatened litigation.
- ☒ Review warranties to ensure they cover all software and services to be provided by the licensor.
- ☒ Beware of general warranty disclaimers that may conflict with express warranties.
- ☒ Require the vendor to "pass through" all relevant third-party warranties.
- ☒ Avoid exclusive remedies for breach of warranty.
- ☒ Always require a vendor intellectual property infringement indemnity and an associated remedy provision.
- ☒ Consider additional vendor indemnities where appropriate (e.g., property damages and personal injury).
- ☒ Limit licensee indemnities to claims for which the licensee is at fault.
- ☒ Make the limitation of liability apply to both parties.
- ☒ Increase the overall liability cap to a multiple of all fees paid.
- ☒ Carve out appropriate exceptions to the limitation of liability (e.g., breach of confidentiality, insured claims, indemnity obligations). Make sure the exceptions to the limitation of liability are carved out of both the exclusion of consequential damages and the overall liability cap.

6

Confidentiality and Security

Two of the most frequently neglected areas in license negotiations are confidentiality and security. While almost every vendor agreement includes a basic confidentiality clause, such clauses are usually one-sided, protecting only the vendor's information. Virtually no vendor license agreements address issues relating to the specific security measures the vendor must implement to protect the licensee's data and other proprietary information while in the vendor's possession. In this chapter, we discuss the protections licensees should require in their vendor agreements to ensure that the licensee's sensitive data and information are held in confidence and adequately protected from authorized access.

The exponential increase in security attacks and breaches in recent years has catapulted cybersecurity to the top of the list of priorities and responsibilities for senior executives and board members. Ensuring appropriate contractual protections are included in all contracts in which third-party vendors will have access to a business' systems and sensitive information is increasingly looked to as an element of compliance by organizations with the evolving standard of care applicable to cybersecurity.

The following sections of the form license agreement are discussed in this Chapter: 6 (Confidentiality).

Confidentiality Provisions

Section 6 of the vendor form agreement illustrates most of the problems found in form vendor agreements. The provision protects only the vendor's information, provides no clear definition of what comprises the "confidential information," and provides none of the standard exceptions to the confidentiality requirements (information that is in the public domain, information that is independently developed by the licensee, etc.). Also, note that Section 6 prevents anyone other than the licensee's own employees from accessing and using the software. If the licensee, for example, permits a contract worker to use the software, it would be in breach of this provision. This type of one-sided confidentiality provision should be rejected. The licensee should insist on a confidentiality provision that satisfies the following requirements:

- The confidentiality obligation should apply to protect the confidential information of both parties.
- A clear, broad definition of "confidential information" should be included. The definition should be carefully reviewed to ensure it includes every type of information the licensee intends to be maintained as confidential.
- The provision should require the receiving party to limit disclosure of the information to employees, contractors, and agents in connection with critical transactions (mergers and acquisitions, significant outsourcing arrangements, and key technology partnerships in which the nature of the relationship with the vendor directly impacts the transaction at issue) who have a need to know and to institute appropriate protections to ensure those individuals understand their obligation to maintain the confidentiality of the information.
- Include standard exceptions (information that is in the public domain, information that is independently developed by the licensee, etc.) to the confidentiality requirement.
- The confidentiality obligations should specifically survive expiration or termination of the agreement; this is particularly important for personally identifiable information of consumers, which should be held in confidence in perpetuity.

In addition to negotiating the language of the confidentiality provision itself, the licensee must ensure breach of the provision is carved out of the limitation of liability.[28] If breach of confidentiality is subject to the limitation of liability, the protections afforded in the confidentiality provision will be rendered largely

[28] *See* Chapter 5 for a discussion of limitation of liability provisions.

useless. If the vendor faces little liability if it breaches its confidentiality obligations, the vendor will have little motivation to take those obligations seriously. Unless it is certain the vendor will have no access to licensee confidential information, the exclusion from the limitation of liability should be aggressively negotiated.

In certain regulated industries (e.g., health care and financial services), the licensee may be under a legal obligation to include additional protections in the confidentiality provision relating to the non-public personally identifiable financial or health care information of its customers. In some cases, a separate agreement relating solely to the protection of personally identifiable information may be required (e.g., a business associate agreement in the health care industry). These provisions require the input of legal counsel experienced in these areas.

If data that is subject to any state, federal, or international law or regulation or if the data constitutes cardholder data under the Payment Card Industry Data Security Standard appropriate additional protections (warranties, indemnities, inclusion of a business associate agreement for protected health information, etc.) should be required. In addition, the common standard used in most confidentiality clauses (i.e., reasonable efforts) should be revised to reflect the application of relevant laws. For example, the following is language found in many vendor form agreements regarding the standard of care for confidentiality: "Each party shall use the same degree of care to prevent disclosure of the other party's Confidential Information as it uses with respect to its own most confidential or proprietary information, which shall not be less than that of a reasonable person under the circumstances."

To reflect the standards imposed by applicable privacy, security, and other laws, that language should be revised as follows:

> Each party shall use the same degree of care to prevent disclosure of the other party's Confidential Information as it uses with respect to its own most confidential or proprietary information, which shall not be less than <u>the standard of care imposed by state and federal laws and regulations relating to the protection of such information and, in the absence of any legally imposed standard of care, the standard shall be</u> that of a reasonable person under the circumstances.

Example Revision:

6. [Alternative No. 1] **Confidentiality.**[29] In the performance of this Agreement, each party may have access to confidential, proprietary, or trade secret information owned or provided by the other party relating to software computer programs, object code, source code, marketing plans, business plans, customers, financial information, specifications, business processes, flow charts, and other data ("Confidential Information"). All Confidential Information supplied by one party to another pursuant to this Agreement shall remain the exclusive property of the disclosing party. The receiving party shall use such Confidential information only for the purposes of this Agreement and shall not copy, disclose, convey, or transfer any of the Confidential Information or any part thereof to any third party, excluding the party's authorized employees and agents. Each party will implement adequate procedures with its employees or other persons permitted or who have access to the Confidential Information to satisfy their obligations under this Agreement. Neither party shall have any obligation with respect to Confidential Information that: (i) is or becomes generally known to the public by any means other than a breach of the obligations of the receiving party; (ii) was previously known to the receiving party or rightly received by the receiving party from a third party; or (iii) is independently developed by or the receiving party.

6. [Alternative No. 2] **Confidentiality.**

6.1 *Confidential Information Defined.* "Confidential Information" shall mean, with respect to a party hereto, all information or material which (i) gives that party some competitive business advantage or the opportunity of obtaining such advantage or the disclosure of which could be detrimental to the interests of that party; or (ii) which is either (A) marked "Confidential," "Restricted," or "Proprietary Information" or other similar marking or (B) known by the parties to be considered confidential and proprietary. Neither party shall have any obligation with respect to confidential information which: (i) is known or used by the receiving party prior to disclosure by the disclosing party; (ii) either before or after the date of the disclosure by the

[29] Suggested replacement language for the existing Section 6 of the vendor form agreement. Alternative No.1 is an example provision of a short form confidentiality provision. Alternative No. 2 presents a more fully fleshed out confidentiality clause.

disclosing party is disclosed to the receiving party by a third party under no obligation of confidentiality to the disclosing party; (iii) either before or after the date of the disclosure to the receiving party becomes published or generally known to the public through no fault of the receiving party; (iv) is independently developed by the receiving party; (v) is required to be disclosed by a final order of a court of competent jurisdiction; or (vi) is otherwise required to be disclosed by applicable law following reasonable notice to the disclosing party.

6.2 *Obligations.* The parties agree to hold each other's Confidential Information in strict confidence. The parties agree not to make each other's Confidential Information available in any form to any third party or to use each other's Confidential Information for any purpose other than as specified in this Agreement. Each party agrees to take all reasonable steps to ensure that Confidential Information of either party is not disclosed or distributed by its employees, agents, or consultants in violation of the provisions of this Agreement. Each party's Confidential Information shall remain the sole and exclusive property of that party. Each party acknowledges that any use or disclosure of the other party's Confidential Information other than as specifically provided for in this Agreement may result in irreparable injury and damage to the non-using or non-disclosing party. Accordingly, each party hereby agrees that, in the event of use or disclosure by the other party other than as specifically provided for in this Agreement, the non-using or non-disclosing party may be entitled to equitable relief as granted by any appropriate judicial body.

Security Provisions

If the vendor will have access to information the licensee classifies as critical (e.g., personally identifiable customer information, highly confidential business information) and will be storing that information on its own servers, in addition to the standard confidentiality provision described above, the licensee should consider including specific contractual requirements relating to the vendor's obligations to secure that information from unauthorized access. These types of requirements can run the gamut from a general "security" provision to additional warranties, indemnities, and lengthy exhibits regarding information handling procedures (e.g., encryption of information in transit, secure disposal of media on which information has been stored, "air-gaping" of critical machines). The size of the transaction and criticality of the data will govern the level of protections required.

While these additional vendor obligations may at first seem onerous and potentially difficult to negotiate, our experience has shown they are generally some of the easier protections to obtain from vendors. Most reputable vendors will likely already have implemented many of the standard security procedures as part of their normal business operations. For example, the vast majority of vendors will likely already use anti-virus software, firewalls, and physical and logical security procedures, monitor their systems for possible intrusions, conduct employee education regarding security, and ensure that access to confidential information is limited to only those employees who have a need to know.

Given that security of data and information will be an issue in most transactions, it is best to raise the issue early with the vendor. We suggest including specific security expectations and requirements in the Request for Proposal (RFP), Request for Information (RFI), or other form of early vendor inquiry used. If an RFP or RFI is not used, the licensee should consider sending the vendor a security questionnaire, requesting information about the prospective vendor's security practices. When completed, the questionnaire should be attached as an exhibit to the agreement and a warranty included by the vendor stating that its responses are true and accurate.

The following is an example of a basic security provision:

Example Provision:

Security Requirements. Vendor will maintain and enforce safety and physical security procedures with respect to its access and maintenance of Customer's Confidential Information that are at least equal to industry standards for such types of locations and that provide reasonably appropriate technical and organizational safeguards against accidental or unlawful destruction, loss, alteration, or unauthorized disclosure or access of Customer Confidential Information. Without limiting the generality of the foregoing, Vendor will take all reasonable measures to secure and defend its location and equipment against "hackers" and others who may seek, without authorization, to modify or access Vendor's systems or the information found therein. Vendor will periodically test its systems for areas where security could potentially be breached. Vendor will immediately report to Customer any breaches of security or unauthorized access to Vendor's systems that Vendor detects or becomes aware of. Vendor will use diligent efforts to remedy such breach of security or unauthorized access in a timely manner and deliver to Customer a root cause assessment and future incident mitigation plan with regard to any breach of security or unauthorized access affecting Customer Confidential Information.

Checklist of Key Issues

The following is a checklist of the key issues presented in this chapter:

- ☒ Unless the vendor will have no exposure to licensee confidential information, always include a mutual confidentiality provision in the license agreement.
- ☒ Ensure that the definition of "confidential information" includes all potential information to be disclosed by the licensee to the vendor.
- ☒ Ensure that the parties' respective employees, contractors, and agents are covered.
- ☒ Ensure that the confidentiality obligation survives any termination or expiration of the agreement.
- ☒ Carve breach of the confidentiality provision out of the limitation of liability.
- ☒ Will the vendor be storing critical licensee information and data on its own servers? If so, consider including specific contractual provisions relating to the vendor's security obligations.

7

Maintenance and Support

In negotiating maintenance and support provisions, the licensee should keep three questions in mind. First, what level of support is needed? Is this a critical application that requires 24X7 support and immediate response from the vendor? Or is this a non-critical application for which a delay by the vendor in responding to a support call will not materially impact the licensee's enterprise? The licensee must assess the impact that a failure in the software will have on its organization and ensure that the support program it is purchasing will adequately address the licensee's requirements. It is on this first question that most licensees focus their negotiation efforts. The remaining two questions, however, are equally important, but frequently left as an afterthought in the negotiation.

The second question the licensee should ask itself in negotiating maintenance and support provisions concerns the licensee's ability to renew support in later years. Most vendor licenses provide no guarantee that the licensee will have support after the initial year of the contract. This is the approach used in Section 3. This means that the licensee could pay to license and install the software and find that it is not able to purchase support after the first year or, worse, that the vendor has abandoned the product. Many licensees have committed this costly mistake.

The final question is, "What is the cost of support during renewal terms?" In most agreements, this issue is not addressed or, as shown in Section 3 of the vendor form agreement, the vendor can simply increase the cost of support at any time without any limitation on the amount of the increase. Such an approach will leave the licensee at the mercy of the vendor after having incurred the cost to license and implement the software. In one case, a licensee paid several hundred thousand dollars to license and implement a piece of software only to have the vendor increase the annual support fees after the first year by a whopping 35 percent.

In this chapter, we discuss approaches to ensuring the licensee can comfortably answer these questions and negotiate reasonable protections in its license agreements.

Beware vendor agreements that fail to provide any real detail about the vendor's support obligations, opting, instead, to reference the details of the support program through a URL. As discussed in Chapter 1, the customer may use various approaches to mitigate the risk of support programs that can change at any time.

The following sections of the form license agreement are discussed in this chapter: 3 (Support and Maintenance).

Support and Maintenance Obligations

Vendors look upon "maintenance and support services" as an exceptionally profitable revenue stream. Generally, maintenance and support services will consist of telephone support and the delivery of software updates, releases, and versions, but in many instances, these "services" are extremely limited, with additional charges for services not included in the basic package. It is important that the licensee clearly define and understand what levels of support it needs and how much it will be charged for that expected level. Otherwise, costs will escalate dramatically from original estimates.

If the software will provide a critical function, the vendor's required response time for various levels of failures (e.g., critical, major, and minor) should be specifically set forth in the support agreement. A remedy (other than breach of contract) should be included to ensure the vendor's compliance with the agreed upon service levels—for example, a credit issued to the licensee for each half-hour or hour that the vendor is late in responding to a critical or major failure.

The licensee should avoid vendor language that requires the licensee to promptly implement all new versions of the software. The licensee may need time to install the new version of the software on a test platform to ensure it operates properly, is compatible with existing systems, and does not pose a security risk, or, more likely, the licensee may desire to delay implementation of a new version until a more convenient time (e.g., it may have received the new version at the end of a quarter, when any interruption in system operation would be unacceptable to the licensee).

With respect to upgrades and modifications to the software, depending on the nature and use of the software, it may be important for the licensee to have the right to test any upgrades before installation and implementation and the right to reject upgrades. In such an event, the vendor should be committed to continue to support the prior version of the software.

Questions to ask when evaluating a vendor's support program include:

- What is included in the support program?
- What are the vendor's normal hours of support?
- Does the vendor provide unlimited telephone support? 24X7 support? Onsite support within two hours when requested? Unlimited user access to support, or will only specified users have access to support?
- Does the vendor provide online discussion forums, frequently asked questions (FAQs), and other support tools?

Example Revision:

3.1 *General Obligations.* Subject to Customer's payment of the annual support fees set forth in Exhibit A, Vendor will provide Customer with reasonable telephone support regarding use and operation of the Licensed Software during the hours of 8 a.m. to 6 p.m. PST, excluding nationally recognized holidays ~~Vendor's normal hours of support~~. Only the current version of the software and immediately preceding version will be supported. Customer must install all new versions of the Licensed Software within six (6) months ~~thirty (30) days~~ of receipt. Vendor reserves the right to charge Customer for support issues that ~~could have been resolved by reference to the Documentation~~[30] ~~or~~ arise from the Customer's failure to use the

[30] Requiring the licensee to pay for support calls because the call could have been avoided if the licensee had more closely read the vendor's documentation is unreasonable and

> ~~negligence, misuse of the~~ Licensed Software as permitted under this Agreement, and issues relating to third-party equipment and software that are not provided or authorized by Vendor. Vendor shall obtain Customer's prior authorization before incurring any such charges. Vendor will provide Customer with any new versions of the Licensed Software that Vendor in its sole discretion makes available to its other licensees at no charge.

Support Term

Support and maintenance services should be structured as having an initial multi-year "Initial Support Term" with a series of optional renewal terms (each a "Renewal Support Term"). This approach has two benefits. First, it locks the vendor into providing support and maintenance for the entire term (both the Initial Support Term and all Renewal Support Terms), while obligating the licensee for only the Initial Support Term. Second, segregating the agreement into an Initial Support Term and a series of Renewal Support Terms provides a basis for fixing the fee for the Initial Support Term and obtaining agreed upon escalations of maintenance and support prices during the Renewal Support Term(s).

Initial Support Terms are usually from three to five years in duration. The number of optional Renewal Support Terms can range from two to five. The important point to remember is that renewal is at the option of the licensee, not the vendor. If the licensee desires to renew support, the vendor must provide it. This ensures that if the licensee goes to the expense of licensing and implementing a piece of software, it will be able to rely on having support for at least a defined number of years (i.e., the Initial Support Term, plus all the optional Renewal Support Terms).

Support Fees

Maintenance and support fees vary widely from vendor to vendor. In general, such fees are calculated as a percentage of the license fees. The percentage can range from 14 percent to 22 percent. A common vendor ploy to increase support fees while appearing to agree to a low percentage is

---

unacceptable. These types of calls are to be expected. If they become excessive, the parties should meet and confer regarding a solution, but the licensee should not be automatically charged for such calls.

to use language such as the following: "Support fees shall be calculated as 16 percent of Vendor's list price for the Licensed Software." This approach should be rejected. Few licensees pay list price for software. Almost all license fees are discounted to some extent. The licensee should require the support fees to be calculated based on the actual license fees paid, not on some substantially higher "list price."

Yearly fees for support should be fixed for at least the first three years of the license term. Thereafter, the licensee should try to negotiate an additional period of one to three years where yearly increases in support fees may not exceed some agreed upon cap (e.g., CPI or CPI plus 3 percent to 7 percent or simply a fixed percentage of the prior year's fees).

A small minority of licensors provide licensees with a "bank of hours" for support (e.g., "Vendor will provide licensee with up to five (5) hours of support in any month of the Term"). Additional hours are charged at a set fee, which the vendor may frequently increase at will. This approach can lead to substantial additional support fees if the bank of hours is exceeded. If the vendor insists on imposing a bank of hours, consider the following negotiating points: use a "stair-step" approach to the bank of hours (e.g., start at 10X, where X is the base monthly bank of hours, during implementation and for six months thereafter, when support calls are likely to be high; after that period, reduce the bank to X hours per month); and exclude all warranty-related calls and product defect calls from the bank of hours, as the licensee should not be required to pay the vendor to fix errors or defects in its own software.

The following example revision shows a potential replacement provision for Section 3.2 of the vendor form agreement that includes the concept of Initial and Renewal Support Terms and price protection.

Example Revision:

3.2 *Support Term and Fees.* Upon the expiration of the initial one- (1-) year support term (the "Initial Support Term"), Customer may, at its option, extend Maintenance and Support for up to five (5) additional consecutive one- (1-) year terms (each a "Renewal Support Term") by providing written notice to Vendor at least thirty (30) days prior to the

> expiration of the pending term, provided that if Customer does not exercise its option to extend at the end of the Initial Support Term, or any Renewal Support Term, the remaining option(s) shall automatically lapse. Vendor shall provide Customer with at least sixty (60) days' prior written notice of the end of the Initial Support Term and each Renewal Support Term. Such notice shall identify any fee increase applicable to the Renewal Support Term that is about to commence. Maintenance and Support fees shall be fixed during the Initial Support Term and first Renewal Support Term. Thereafter, Vendor may increase such fees for a Renewal Support Term by providing notice to Customer at least sixty (60) days prior to the commencement of such term. Any such increase shall not exceed the lesser of: (i) four percent (4%) of the fees charged during the preceding term; or (ii) Vendor's then current generally applicable rates, less fifteen percent (15%).

Checklist of Key Issues

The following is a checklist of the key issues presented in this chapter:

- ☒ Is the support program described in the agreement or referenced through a URL?
- ☒ Confirm the vendor's support program satisfies the licensee's performance requirements (hours of support, call response times, testing of new releases, etc.).
- ☒ Draft the term of support to provide for an initial term and renewal terms, at the licensee's sole option.
- ☒ Fix support fees for the first several years of the agreement, and cap fee increases in later years.
- ☒ Reject attempts by vendors to limit support calls to a "bank" of hours.
- ☒ Allow sufficient time to implement new releases (e.g., six months from the release date).
- ☒ Limit the vendor's ability to include "tack-on" support fees (charges for out-of-scope support calls, fees for onsite service to fix inherent bugs in the software, etc.)

8

Miscellaneous License Provisions

The chapter presents a discussion of a number of miscellaneous provisions in the vendor form agreement. In addition, we have included several additional "specialty" provisions (e.g., source code escrow, publicity, reference cite) for potential inclusion in appropriate transactions. While these provisions are characterized as miscellaneous license provisions, this should in no way diminish their importance. The reader should be familiar with each of these provisions and its use.

The following sections of the form license agreement are discussed in this chapter: 1 (Definitions), 2.5 (Ownership), 2.6 (Feedback), 2.10 (Aggregated Data), 11.3 (Limitation of Actions), 17 (Entire Agreement), 19 (Assignment), and 24 (Publicity).

Defined Terms

Licensors often incorporate important material in definitions. If each definition is not read carefully and fully understood, the licensee may inadvertently agree to something that does not reflect its understanding and intent. We have already discussed this issue in the context of the definition of "Licensed Software" in Chapter 3 and the definition of "Documentation" in Chapter 4. Other important definitions appearing frequently in vendor agreements include the definition of "Licensee"; the definition of "Authorized Uses," referring to the uses to which the software may be put by the licensee; if the software will be installed on a particular server or at a specific location, the definition of that server or location should be carefully reviewed; the definition of "Acceptance"; and the definition of "Support and Maintenance" and the related definitions of "support hours" and software "bug" or "error."

Ownership, Feedback, and Aggregated Data

Section 2.5 of the vendor form agreement is a provision commonly found in most vendor agreements. It is so common that it is frequently glossed over without serious review. Among other things, the licensee should consider the following points in reviewing these types of provisions.

The licensee should not agree or acknowledge that the vendor owns anything. Rather, the licensee should take the position that the vendor has whatever rights it may have under existing intellectual property law, but agree to nothing further. The licensee should certainly not agree to any language along the lines that the licensee will never "contest" or take any action "contrary" to the vendor's intellectual property rights. There are two reasons for taking this position. First, if the vendor ever alleges that the licensee's use of the software infringes its intellectual property rights, the licensee will likely defend the suit, in part, by arguing that the vendor has no enforceable intellectual property rights. The language in Section 2.5 of the vendor agreement would undermine the licensee's ability to take that position (i.e., the licensee has already agreed in writing that it will never contest the vendor's intellectual property rights).

The second reason for objecting to this type of language is the possibility that the licensee could hold the intellectual property rights in certain patents, trade secrets, or copyrights that could be embodied in the current or some future version of the software. Consider the following example. The licensee holds a patent in a particular form of technology used to search large volumes of text. The licensee purchases a piece of software that provides general office productivity applications. A subsequent release includes the ability to search all text on the licensee's hard disk. The new search capability directly infringes the licensee's patent. Can the licensee enforce its patent against the licensor? In the absence of the license agreement, the answer would be an emphatic yes. With the license agreement, the answer is unclear or, worse, no. If the licensee has stipulated that the licensor owns all the intellectual property rights in the software and has further agreed never to contest those rights or do anything contrary to them, the licensee may find itself in breach of contract if it sues the licensor for infringing its patent.

Another important point to look for and avoid in ownership provisions is a broad statement that the vendor owns all derivative works based on the licensed software. The problem with such a provision is that almost anything that interacts with the software could arguably be a derivative work. But consider the case where a licensee interfaces one of its proprietary applications with the licensed software. Has the licensee created a derivative work? Possibly. If a derivative work has been created, the licensee may have just assigned the rights in its own proprietary application to the vendor.

Finally, to avoid any possibility that the vendor may claim ownership of all or any portion of the licensee's intellectual property, a clear and unequivocal statement to that effect should be included in *every* license agreement.

The foregoing issues are addressed in the example revision below:

Example Revision:

2.5 *Ownership*. This Agreement does not grant to Customer any ownership interest in the Licensed Software. Rather, Customer has a license to use the Licensed Software as provided in this Agreement. ~~Customer hereby agrees and acknowledges that~~ Vendor owns all right, title, and interest in the Licensed Software ~~and Customer will not contest those rights or engage in any conduct contrary to those rights~~. Any copy, modification, revision, enhancement, adaptation, translation, or derivative work of or created from the Software by Vendor ~~made by or at the direction of Customer~~ shall be owned solely and exclusively by Vendor, as shall all patent rights, copyrights, trade secret rights, trademark rights, and all other proprietary rights, worldwide (all of the foregoing rights taken together being referred to collectively herein as "Intellectual Property Rights") therein and thereto. ~~Customer hereby irrevocably assigns and transfers to Vendor all of Customer's Intellectual Property Rights in the foregoing.~~ Notwithstanding the foregoing or any other provision of this Agreement, nothing contained herein shall be construed as granting Vendor any right, title, or interest in or to any of Customer's intellectual property or Confidential Information.

Many vendor agreements contain two other provisions that may affect the customer's intellectual property rights: feedback and aggregated data.

A feedback provision permits the vendor to use input, suggestions, comments, etc., provided by the customer to improve the vendor's products. There is nothing fundamentally wrong with such a provision. Problems arise, however, when those provisions are written too expansively and, even, contain broad assignments of intellectual property rights from the customer to the vendor. Worse, there have been instances where a customer suggests new functionality to a vendor, which the vendor implements, and then the vendor claims compensation from the customer when that functionality becomes the subject of an intellectual property infringement claim. The customer should have no liability whatsoever for the feedback it provides. It is up to the vendor to properly vet the feedback it receives.

Example Revision:

2.6 *Feedback.* Customer may provide suggestions, comments, or other feedback (collectively, "Feedback") to Vendor with respect to its products and services, including the Licensed Software. Feedback is voluntary. Provider may use Feedback for any purpose without obligation of any kind. <u>All Feedback is provided by Customer entirely as-is, without warranties of any kind. All use of Feedback is at Vendor's sole risk and liability.</u> ~~Customer hereby irrevocably assigns and transfers to Vendor all of Customer's Intellectual Property Rights in the Feedback.~~

Aggregated data provisions provide the vendor with the right to derive statistical and other data regarding the performance and use of its software. The vendor may use the data to improve its products and, potentially, sell the data to other customers. As with feedback clauses, there is nothing fundamentally wrong with such a provision. The key is ensuring the aggregated data clause requires the vendor to aggregate the data so that it is not identifiable or capable of re-identification to the customer or any other individual or entity. The clause must also make clear that the customer will have no liability for the aggregated data (i.e., if the vendor fails to de-identify the data properly and causes the customer to be sued, the customer should be indemnified against that claim).

Example Revision (Replace Section 2.10):

<u>2.10 Customer hereby grants Vendor a non-exclusive, "as-is," perpetual, royalty-free license to use Aggregated Data (defined below) in connection with its business. "Aggregated Data" refers to data derived from</u>

Customer's use of the Licensed Software that is combined with other similar data of Vendor's other customers. Aggregated Data shall not include (directly or by inference) any (i) information identifying Customer or any identifiable customer or individual or capable of re-identification to the foregoing; (ii) Customer Confidential Information; or (iii) Customer intellectual property. The foregoing shall not be construed as a representation or warranty by Customer that it has the rights, if any, to grant such license or to authorize such use. Vendor acknowledges and agrees that the Aggregated Data is provided by Customer as-is, without warranties of any kind. Customer hereby disclaims all warranties, express and implied, including the implied warranties of merchantability, fitness for a particular purpose, title/non-infringement, and quality of information with regard to the Aggregated Data. Vendor shall defend, indemnify, and hold harmless Customer and its directors, officers, agents, employees, members, subsidiaries, and successors in interest from and against any claim, action, proceeding, liability, loss, damage, cost, or expense, including, without limitation, attorneys' fees, experts' fees, and court costs as provided herein arising out of or relating to (i) the license granted in this Section; (ii) Vendor's failure to properly and adequately remove all entity and personally identifiable information from the Aggregated Data; or (iii) any claims resulting from Vendor's use, distribution, sale, licensing, or other exploitation of the Aggregated Data.

Limitation of Actions

The limitation of actions, or "statute of limitations," provision imposes a contractual limitation on the period within which a party may bring a lawsuit against the other party. These provisions are used to circumvent the normal period under applicable law that a party would have to file a suit. For example, in many jurisdictions, the period within which a party must bring an action for breach of contract is four years from the date of the breach. Section 11.3 of the vendor form agreement would change that period to one year. Also, note that Section 11.3 applies only to claims by the customer. While the licensee may feel comfortable putting some limit on the length of time within which a lawsuit must be brought, that limit should generally not be less than two or three years. In addition, the licensee should insist that any limitation of actions provision apply equally to both parties.

Example Revision:

11.3 *Limitation of Actions.* <u>Neither party</u> ~~Customer~~ shall ~~not~~ bring any action against <u>the other party</u> ~~Vendor~~ arising out of or related to this Agreement or the subject matter hereof more than <u>three</u> ~~one~~ (~~1~~<u>3</u>) year<u>s</u> after the occurrence of the event which gave rise to such action.

Force Majeure

Most vendor-drafted agreements include what is known as a *force majeure* clause. This clause was originally designed to excuse parties of their contractual obligations in the event of certain acts of God, such as fire, earthquake, or civil disturbance. Over the years, however, vendors have expanded the meaning of "*force majeure*" well beyond its intended purpose to include such events as interruption of communication service, employee relation difficulties, and any act "beyond the Licensor's control." This is not an acceptable allocation of risk, especially when the software and services being provided by the vendor are critical to the licensee's business operations. If the vendor demands some type of protection, the *force majeure* provision should be limited to true acts of God, and an extended delay should trigger a termination right for the licensee. In addition, if the licensee has any obligations with regard to implementation of the software, the provision should be made applicable to both parties.

Another revision to consider is an equitable adjustment in fees due from the customer to reflect the period of non-performance. That is, performance may not be entirely disrupted by the *force majeure* event. The vendor could, for example, perform some, but not all, services. In that case, the following language may be included: "For the avoidance of doubt, if Vendor's performance hereunder is the subject of a *force majeure* event, the fees to be paid by Customer shall be equitably adjusted to reflect the period in which Vendor's performance was affected."

Example Revision:

15. ***Force Majeure***. Vendor shall not be responsible for failures of its obligations under this Agreement to the extent that such failure is due to causes beyond Vendor's control, including, but not limited to, acts of God,

> war, acts of any government or agency thereof, fire, explosions, epidemics, and quarantine restrictions~~, strikes, delivery services, telecommunication providers, strikes, labor difficulties, lockouts, embargoes, severe weather conditions, delay in transportation, or delay of suppliers or subcontractors~~. If the suspension of Vendor's performance continues for more than fourteen (14) days, Customer may terminate this Agreement effective immediately.

Integration Clause

Integration provisions such as the one in Section 17 of the vendor form agreement are standard in contracts and generally serve to protect both parties. The concept is, "If it is not in this agreement, it does not exist." Thus, neither party can assert that it said something to the contrary, was told something different, was promised something not in the agreement, etc. It is imperative for the licensee to understand, however, that if a representation was made to the licensee regarding software performance or functionality, and that representation is not included in the agreement, it is as if that representation had never been made. Consequently, all documents containing licensor representations or other things upon which the licensee is relying must be incorporated into or attached to the agreement. To the extent the licensor has made oral representations regarding important software performance capabilities or functions, those statements should be reduced to writing, and, after the licensor has had an opportunity to review the representations, they should be incorporated into, or attached as, an exhibit.

In addition to ensuring that all information and documentation on which the licensee is relying in entering into the transaction are incorporated into the license agreement, language should be added to the license agreement to prevent it from being overridden by, for example, shrink-wrap license agreements provided with the delivery disks.

Another potential area of concern is the vendor's privacy policy taking precedence over the confidentiality and other obligations in the negotiated agreement between the parties. If personally identifiable information of consumers will be at risk, the protective language regarding shrink-wrap and other similar agreements should specifically reference privacy policies.

Example Revision:

17. ***Entire Agreement.*** This Agreement constitutes the entire agreement between the parties with respect to the subject matter hereof and supersedes all other prior and contemporary agreements, understandings, and commitments between the parties regarding the subject matter of this Agreement. This Agreement may not be modified or amended except by a written instrument executed by the parties. In particular, any provisions, terms, or conditions contained in Customer's Purchase Orders or other similar forms that are in any way inconsistent with or in addition to the terms and conditions of this Agreement shall not be binding upon Vendor. No shrink-wrap, click-wrap, privacy policy, or other terms and conditions or agreements ("Additional Terms") provided with any products, services, documentation, or software hereunder shall be binding on Customer, even if use of the foregoing requires an affirmative "acceptance" of those Additional Terms before access is permitted. All such Additional Terms shall be of no force or effect and shall be deemed rejected by Customer in their entirety.

Assignment

Almost every vendor agreement includes a strict prohibition on the licensee's right to assign the agreement, even in the event of a merger or acquisition. In the event of such an occurrence, the successor entity may have to spend hundreds of thousands, potentially millions, of dollars re-licensing software used by the acquired entity. These types of provisions are unfair to the licensee and may result in a windfall to the licensor.

The licensee should require the ability to assign its rights under the agreement to its affiliates and other entities that may become successors or affiliates through reorganization, consolidation, divestiture, and the like. Any concerns the vendor may have from an assignment can be addressed by the requirement that the assignee will accept all of the licensee's obligations under the agreement. Similarly, the licensee should also obtain assurance that any vendor assignee will agree to be bound by all of the terms and conditions of the agreement, including, without limitation, maintenance and support obligations.

Example Revision:

19. ***Assignment***. <u>Except as provided below,</u> neither this Agreement nor any interest in this Agreement may be assigned by <u>either party</u> ~~Customer~~ without the prior express of written approval of <u>the other party, and such approval shall not be unreasonably withheld or delayed</u> ~~Vendor~~. ~~Vendor may assign, pledge, mortgage, sell to a third party, or otherwise dispose of all or any portion of this Agreement, provided that such action shall not relieve Vendor of its obligations to Customer under this Agreement or reduce Customer's rights hereunder.~~ <u>Notwithstanding the foregoing, either party may assign this Agreement to an affiliate or to a successor entity in the event of a merger, acquisition, or sale of all or substantially all of its assets. Any such successor entity shall agree in writing to be bound by the terms of this Agreement.</u>

19. ***Assignment***.[31] This Agreement shall not be assigned by either party without the prior written consent of the other, except as follows:

    A. Vendor may assign this Agreement provided (i) such assignment is in writing; (ii) such assignment states that the assignee is accepting all obligations of Vendor under this Agreement and agrees to be bound by and discharge the Agreement's terms, conditions, and obligations as if it were the original party hereto; and (iii) Vendor, the assignee entity, or both agree in writing to support the Licensed Software throughout the Term.

    B. Customer may assign this Agreement to a parent or subsidiary corporation, a subsidiary of its parent corporation, or any corporation or entity in which Customer has an ownership interest, or in the event of an affiliation, merger, acquisition, sale or disposition of substantially all of its assets, consolidation, or other joint operating arrangement between Customer and a third party(ies), provided such assignment (i) is in writing and (ii) states that the assignee is accepting all obligations of Customer under this Agreement and agrees to be bound by and discharge each of the Agreement's terms, conditions, and obligations as if it were the original party hereto.

---

[31] The following is an alternate, more fully fleshed-out version of the assignment provision.

Source Code Escrow

With particularly important or critical software, it may be necessary to require the vendor to deposit the source code of the software with a third-party escrow company. This permits the licensee to obtain the source code for the purpose of supporting, maintaining, and modifying the software if the vendor fails to provide support and maintenance, for example, because of the vendor's bankruptcy or a decision by a purchaser of the vendor to stop supporting the software.

There are two types of source code escrow agreements: two-party and three-party. Two-party agreements are by far the most common. In a two-party arrangement, the licensor has established a single, general escrow for the benefit of all of its licensees. Additional licensees are added as beneficiaries of the escrow by signing a simple one- or two-page form. Three-party agreements are escrow agreements created specifically for a given transaction and are signed by the licensee, the licensor, and the escrow agent. Three-party escrow agreements are not common.

A common error in source code escrow provisions is to have the source code treated exactly as the licensed software, with no change in the uses to which the software can be put. The correct approach is to expand the scope of the license to permit the licensee to provide its own support and to modify the source code.

Example Provision:

24. **Escrow of Source Materials**

24.1 *Escrow Agent and Release Conditions.* Vendor has deposited a copy of the Source Material (as defined below) for the Licensed Software with ______________________________, a software escrow agent (the "Escrow Agent"), located at ____________________, __________ (the "Escrow"), pursuant to a written Escrow Agreement. During the Term, Vendor shall continually update the Source Material by promptly depositing in the escrow each new release, update, version, enhancement, correction, patch, and improvement of the Licensed Software.

24.2 *Use of Source Material.* Upon the occurrence of a Release Condition (as defined in the Escrow Agreement), Customer will, upon payment of the duplication cost and other handling charges of the Escrow Agent, be entitled to obtain a copy of such Source Material from the Escrow Agent. Customer shall be entitled to use the Source Material as needed to remedy the event of release and mitigate any damages arising from such event. Such use will include, but is not limited to, Customer's right to perform its own support and maintenance and alter or modify the Source Material. Nothing herein relieves Vendor of its obligation to provide support as required under this Agreement.

24.3 *Customer's Right to Verify Source Material.* Regardless of whether one of the Release Conditions occurs, Customer shall have the right, at Customer's sole expense, to require the Escrow Agent to verify the relevance, completeness, currency, accuracy, and functionality of the Source Material by, among other things, compiling the Source Material and performing test runs for comparison with the capabilities of the Licensed Software. If such testing demonstrates that the Source Material does not correspond to the Licensed Software, Vendor shall reimburse Customer for all costs and fees incurred in the testing and immediately deposit the correct Source Material with the Escrow Agent.

24.4 *Source Material—Defined.* For purposes of this Agreement, "Source Material" shall mean, with respect to the Licensed Software, the source code of such software and all related compiler command files, build scripts, scripts relating to the operation and maintenance of such application, application programming interface (API), graphical user interface (GUI), object libraries, all relevant instructions on building the object code of such application, and all documentation relating to the foregoing, such that collectively the foregoing will be sufficient to enable a person possessing reasonable skill and expertise in computer software and information technology to build, load, and operate the machine-executable object code of such application, to maintain and support such application, and to effectively use all functions and features of such software.

24.5 *Fee.* There shall be no charge to Customer for the maintenance of the Escrow under this Agreement.

Change Control

If the vendor will be providing implementation services, the license agreement should address the change control and change order procedure.

Generally, the longer a project is anticipated to last, the more likely changes will be required. The contract should have a defined procedure that addresses the mechanism for either party proposing changes to the scope; documenting the impact of those changes on the contract price, schedule, personnel, or other aspect of the contract; and accepting or modifying the change in scope. A very basic change order provision is shown below.

Example Provision:

25. ***Change Orders***. Either party may submit a written change request to the other party for consideration. On receiving each change request, the parties shall meet and confer regarding the request, the availability of Vendor's staff, cost of any changes, and any impact the change will have on project scheduling and product warranties or other obligations under this Agreement. If the parties agree to the change, the written change order will be signed by both parties and attached as an exhibit to this Agreement.

Potential Outsourcing

In today's business environment, many licensees will desire to have a third-party outsourcing partner provide some or all of its information technology operations. In particular, the licensee may desire to have a third-party host and provide access to a software application. If outsourcing is or will be a possibility in the near future, the licensee should include a specific right to outsource in the license agreement. Raising this issue early with the vendor and ensuring that it is addressed in the agreement will avoid later disputes and potential additional fees. The following is an example of such an outsourcing provision:

Example Provision:

26. **Outsourcing and Customer's Designee**

26.1 *Customer's Designee.* Any third-party outsourcing vendor, contractor, agent, or other person or entity designated by Customer in writing (the "Customer Designee") shall be entitled to enforce and/or perform any responsibilities, obligations, or other provisions attributed to Customer under this Agreement. Customer shall provide the Vendor with written notice of the

Customer Designee, including the general scope and nature of the authority of the Customer Designee (the "Designee Authority Letter").

26.2 *Vendor Cooperation*. Vendor shall fully cooperate with, communicate with, coordinate with, and respond to all the requests of the Customer Designee within the general scope and nature of the authority of the Customer Designee. Such cooperation will include Vendor's participation at meetings with such other vendor(s) covering technical, operational, or planning matters relating to Vendor's services and such other vendor's services.

26.3 *Approvals*. Vendor shall be entitled to reasonably rely on the Customer Designee, provided, however, that Customer Approval shall be required for any work effort requested by a Customer Designee that is reasonably anticipated to result in fees and/or expenses not already documented in the Agreement. Customer shall be entitled to amend and/or terminate its use of the Customer Designee at any time upon advance notice to Vendor. Customer will require each Customer Designee to enter into an agreement containing appropriate confidentiality and non-use provisions with respect to Vendor Confidential Information. Customer shall remain responsible to Vendor for any performance required under this Agreement by Customer.

26.4 *Existing or Successor Outsourcer*. For purposes of this Agreement, XYZ Corporation ("Outsourcer") shall be a Customer Designee. The general scope and nature of the authority of Outsourcer with regard to Vendor includes the following:

1. Work with Customer to plan the scope, requirements, and specifications for any particular project or engagement;
2. Assume responsibility for properly fulfilling Customer's operational, management, and administrative obligations under any agreement with Vendor;
3. Work with Customer to identify its business needs and assume primary responsibility for incorporating those business needs in the design and development of specifications for the Vendor's services;
4. Act as Customer's limited agent and coordinate the implementation of Vendor projects and performance;
5. Assume responsibility for managing the relationship and monitoring Vendor's continuing performance under the terms of this Agreement, and bring all performance issues under the applicable service levels to resolution in accordance with the terms of this Agreement, including, but not limited to, oversight of Vendor's development and implementation of corrective action plans;

6. Monitor Vendor's continuing timeliness of performance under the terms of this Agreement;
7. Monitor and assess Vendor's ability to efficiently and effectively deliver the agreed services under the terms of this Agreement ; and
8. Review and verify the accuracy of and compliance with the terms of this Agreement by Vendor. Customer may, in its sole discretion, elect to outsource its remaining, non-financial obligations as to the operation of all or any portion of the Licensed Software.

There shall be no additional license fees, transfer fees, or other fees paid by Customer to Vendor in connection with any outsourcing election hereunder, regardless of any site or central processing unit (CPU) transfer(s). Any such outsourcing vendor(s) shall agree to comply with the confidentiality provisions of this Agreement.

Use of Licensee's Name and Referral Sites

Many vendors will request permission to use the licensee's name as a reference and in connection with its promotional materials. In addition, the vendor may request that the licensee commit to serving as a reference site for potential new customers. While the licensee may be willing to lend use of its name to the vendor, it should refrain from providing a blanket commitment to serve as a reference site. Such activities can require the licensee to spend valuable personnel time entertaining potential customers of the vendor. In addition, the licensee will be required to admit third parties to its facilities to view operation of the licensed software on its systems. Such intrusive activities should be strictly limited. In any event, the commitment to allow onsite demonstrations should not be given without receiving some additional concession from the vendor (e.g., free training, a bank of professional service hours, price breaks on support).

Section 24 of the vendor agreement in Chapter 1 provides an example of a typical, overreaching vendor request to use the customer's name and trademarks. That language should be either deleted or replaced with a more reasonable provision, such as that shown below.

Example Provision:

24. **Demonstrations and Promotions**

24.1 *Promotions Referring to Customer.* The parties agree that Vendor may use a textual reference (i.e., no use of Customer logos and/or other materials) to Customer in its client list and other materials. However, Vendor agrees that Customer shall be entitled to review and approve any promotional materials that contain a reference to Customer as contemplated herein before publication or distribution of same. No more than once each year of the Term, Customer agrees to permit one on-site demonstration of Vendor's software to a prospective customer. All such on-site demonstrations shall be scheduled at a time acceptable to Customer, and no third party will be granted access to Customer's facilities without first executing Customer's then current non-disclosure agreement. Notwithstanding the foregoing, Customer shall be under no obligation to grant access to its facilities to any competitor of Customer.

24.2 *Demonstration and Promotions Not Warranties.* In no event shall any demonstration or any promotional materials pursuant to this Section constitute an endorsement, representation, or warranty, express or implied, by Customer, with respect to the Licensed Software. In the event of a dispute between Customer and Vendor, Customer's agreement to participate in promotions and demonstrations under this Section and all statements made by Customer in connection with such activities shall not be deemed an admission or declaration against interest of Customer in any trial or dispute resolution proceeding between the parties.

Access to Licensee Facilities

If the vendor will be rendering implementation or other services at the licensee's facilities, the licensee should consider including a provision regarding how access will be made and the vendor's obligations while at the licensee's facilities.

Example Provision:

27. ***Access to Customer Facilities.*** Vendor, its employees and agents, will be granted access to Customer facilities subject to Vendor's prior notification to Customer and compliance with Customer's standard

> administrative and security requirements, for the purpose of executing Vendor's obligations hereunder. Access to Customer facilities shall be restricted to normal Customer business hours, 6:30 a.m. to 6:30 p.m., Monday through Friday, Customer-observed holidays excepted. Access to Customer facilities outside normal business hours must be approved in writing in advance by Customer, which approval will not be unreasonably withheld. Vendor shall have no tenancy or any other property or other rights in Customer facilities. While present at Customer facilities, Vendor's personnel shall be accompanied by Customer personnel at all times, unless otherwise specified in writing prior to such event by Customer's Project Director. All Vendor personnel shall conduct themselves at all times in a professional manner and wear appropriate work attire.

Insurance

In appropriate instances, the licensee should require the vendor to provide evidence of insurance, to maintain that insurance throughout the term of the agreement, and to notify the licensee of any changes to the insurance. Insurance provisions are important to ensure that the licensee has a level of comfort and protection that if things go badly, the licensee will be able to recover money damages against the vendor.

> **Example Provision:**
>
> 28. **Insurance Requirements**[32]
>
> 28.1 *Required Insurance Coverages.* Vendor shall obtain, pay for, and maintain in full force and effect during the Term insurance as follows:
>
> A. Statutory California Workers' Compensation coverage including all-states endorsement. Employer's Liability coverage for one million dollars ($1,000,000) per occurrence for all employees engaged in services or operations under this Agreement;

---

[32] The liability limits mentioned in this provision are offered as examples only. The actual limits in a particular contract will be governed by the amount of fees involved in that transaction and the criticality of the application to the licensee's organization.

B. Commercial general liability insurance with limits of three million dollars ($3,000,000) aggregate for bodily injury, death, and property damage, including personal injury, contractual liability, independent contractors, broad-form property damage, and products and completed operations coverage;

C. Automobile liability insurance with limits of one million dollars ($1,000,000) each occurrence combined single limit of liability for bodily injury, death, and property damage, including owned and non-owned and hired automobile coverages, as applicable; and

D. Professional Liability Insurance (Errors and Omissions) with limits of three million dollars ($3,000,000) each occurrence. Annual aggregate for all claims each policy year for computer programming and electronic data processing services.

Generally, cybersecurity insurance would be more relevant in a hosted engagement, not locally installed software where the vendor won't have possession of company data.

28.2 *Claims-Made Coverages.* To the extent any insurance coverage required under this Section is purchased on a "claims-made" basis, such insurance shall cover all prior acts of Vendor during the Term, and such insurance shall be continuously maintained until at least three (3) years beyond the expiration or termination of this Agreement, or Vendor shall purchase "tail" coverage, effective upon termination of any such policy or upon termination or expiration of this Agreement, to provide coverage for at least one (1) year from the occurrence of either such event.

28.3 *Certificates of Insurance.* Prior to the Effective Date, Vendor shall provide to Customer an original and one copy of a Certificate of Insurance certifying that coverage as described in this Section has been obtained. The verification of insurance coverage shall be sent to the address indicated. The Certificate of Insurance shall state:

A. Customer, its officers, agents, and employees as additional insureds (required for Commercial General Liability and Automobile Liability only);

B. That each of the policies is primary insurance with respect to any other insurance available to Customer as to any claim for which coverage is afforded under the policy; and

C. That the policy shall apply separately to each insured against whom a claim is made or suit is brought (required for Commercial General Liability and Automobile Liability only).

28.4 *Subcontractors to Be Insured.* Vendor shall require all of its subcontractors to carry insurance coverages and limits as agreed to and approved in writing by Customer.

28.5 *Cancellation or Lapse of Insurance.* Vendor shall provide thirty (30) days' prior written notice to Customer of cancellation. Should Vendor fail to keep in effect at all times the insurance coverages required under this Section, Customer may, in addition to and cumulative with any other remedies available at law, equity, or hereunder, terminate this Agreement.

Training

Licensees should not overlook the issue of training in their license negotiations. Almost every application will require training from the vendor in its use and operation. The cost of that training should be set in the negotiation of the license agreement. Since this is an additional revenue stream for the vendor, the licensee should consider locking rates for ongoing training, including training for new releases and versions of the software.

Most licensees elect a "train the trainer" approach in which they send a number of personnel to the vendor for training so that they may return to the licensee's organization and train the licensee's remaining personnel. To ensure training is adequate, the vendor should be required to identify specifically the training and associated cost required to become knowledgeable in the operation of the software. To avoid hidden costs, the licensee may even go so far as to require a warranty from the vendor to the effect that the identified training will be sufficient to train a user in the operation and use of the software. In evaluating the vendor's training program, the licensee should consider requesting copies of the vendor's training materials and talk to existing vendor customers.

Documentation

In many instances, licensees may want to create copies of the vendor's documentation for distribution within its own organization. Moreover, the licensee may want to create its own documentation for its personnel based on the vendor's documentation (e.g., by excerpting relevant portions from the vendor's documentation). To avoid hidden costs associated with the foregoing, the licensee should specifically request these rights from the vendor.

Example Provision:

29. **Documentation**. During the Term and at no additional charge to Customer (except applicable shipping costs), Vendor shall provide Customer with all Documentation relating to the Licensed Software. If the Documentation for the Licensed Software is revised or supplemented at any time during the Term, Vendor shall promptly deliver a copy of such revised or supplemental Documentation to Customer, at no additional cost to Customer (except applicable shipping costs). Customer may, at any time, reproduce copies of all Documentation and other materials provided by Vendor, distribute such copies to its personnel, and incorporate such copies into its own technical manuals, provided that such reproduction relates to Customer's use of the Licensed Software, and copyright notices, if any, are reproduced thereon. Vendor shall deliver to Customer one (1) electronic copy of each available, standard version of Vendor's user Documentation for each item of Licensed Software, to the extent available (the "Electronic Copy"). Customer is hereby authorized to make and use derivative works ("Derivatives") of the works contained on the Electronic Copy and to make and use physical copies of the Derivatives, and to deliver such copies only to its personnel, subject to the confidentiality provisions contained herein.

Checklist of Key Issues

The following is a checklist of the key issues presented in this chapter:

- ☒ Carefully check the definitions of all defined terms.
- ☒ Ensure the ownership provision does not adversely affect the licensee's ability to protect its own intellectual property or prejudice its rights in a potential litigation with the vendor.
- ☒ Limit overly expansive feedback and aggregated data provisions to ensure protection of the licensee's intellectual property and data.

☒ Limitation of actions provisions should be made applicable to both parties, and the limitation period should not be less than two or three years.

☒ *Force majeure* provisions should not be a "get out of jail free card" for vendors. These provisions should be limited to true acts of God and should include a termination right for the licensee in the event of prolonged interruptions in service.

☒ Integration clauses limit the "deal" to the four corners of the license agreement. If the licensee is relying on any oral representations by the vendor or any vendor documentation, those items should be specifically incorporated into the agreement.

☒ Include language to avoid later shrink-wrap agreements from conflicting with or overriding the license agreement.

☒ The license agreement is a valuable asset of the licensee. As such, the licensee should have a right to assign the agreement to a successor entity or an affiliate.

☒ If the software provides critical functionality to the licensee, the licensee should consider requiring the vendor to place the source code for the software into escrow with a third party.

☒ If the licensor will be providing implementation services, include a change control provision to address later changes in the scope of those services.

☒ If the licensee is contemplating outsourcing all or any portion of its information technology infrastructure, it should include a specific provision in the license permitting outsourcing of the application to licensee's third-party designate and stating that there will be no additional license, support, or other fees associated with the outsourcing.

☒ Avoid broad commitments to serve as a referral site for the vendor. Require that all marketing materials containing the licensee's name be submitted to the licensee for approval.

☒ If the vendor will have access to the licensee's facilities, the vendor should be required to schedule all visits in advance with the licensee and comply with the licensee's access and security requirements.

9

Managing Technology Across the Enterprise

"Misdirected" is the nicest description of the manner in which most enterprises approach software licensing and technology services contracting and management. In this chapter, we will discuss the importance of an enterprise information technology management process and provide a detailed blueprint for creating an effective contracting and management process within your enterprise.

In many enterprises, responsibility for the procurement, structuring, and implementation of software licenses is still diffused among various departments, though increasingly, the responsibility is concentrated in the supply chain organization. Regardless of the department that drives the process, the lines of responsibility for decision-making in the process are frequently blurred among supply chain, information technology, legal, finance, or the business unit sponsoring the technology initiative. These lines of responsibility are often redrawn in connection with each new technology initiative.

Each department within the organization has its own key "issues" that it seeks to have addressed, but frequently, the appreciation among the departments for the issues of the other departments is not as good as it could or should be. Most important, the absence of engagement by individuals with an appreciation of the "end to end" software licensing issues from the beginning of the initiative affects the quality of the end product. Significantly, the siloed issue responsibility, diffused accountability, and knowledge within the enterprise can lead to significant disaffection of one or more departments with the process and may cause a particular technology initiative to proceed without the benefit of the full and informed input from important participants within the enterprise.

We have seen scenarios similar to the above in organizations of all types and sizes. Our view is that one of the primary causes for these issues is the failure of an enterprise to (1) take a holistic view of the software licensing and technology services procurement, structuring and negotiation, and implementation processes and (2) utilize a procurement model to consistently deliver a holistic approach and effectively manage those processes both within their organization and with the vendor.

The lack of such a coherent process leads enterprises to the following adverse results:

- The failure to identify hidden costs, liabilities, and business risks associated with a software license;
- The failure to protect critical company assets;
- Duplication of effort;
- Inability to harness important corporate knowledge and establish uniform business practices; and
- Inefficient and ineffective procurement processes.

Conversely, implementation of an enterprise information technology management process in which business processes and tools are used to create an enterprise-specific, best-practice approach to software licensing and technology services procurement provides opportunities for the enterprise to:

- Materially reduce its technology costs across the enterprise by leveraging buying power and technology procurement and negotiation expertise;
- Improve the likelihood that corporate objectives identified in support of a specific technology initiative will be achieved;
- Improve integration and flow of information throughout the enterprise and to interested corporate stakeholders;
- Streamline, rationalize, and improve the technology procurement cycle (enabling the organization to shorten the time between approval of concept and realization of objectives);

- Minimize data security, privacy, and liability exposure; and
- Minimize the likelihood of failure, as well as the business impacts in the event of a failure.

While each of the above is a compelling reason for rationalizing the information technology processes within your enterprise, the high cost of technology failures and the need to minimize the likelihood and business impacts of such failures alone justify the effort to re-examine these processes. A system failure can have severely adverse implications on customer service/fulfillment issues, result in lost revenue and loss of competitive advantages, adversely impact your company's reputation, create significant and unbudgeted correction costs, result in security or privacy breaches or regulatory non-compliance creating additional liabilities, and may impact staff retention and create recruiting challenges.

In addition to the often recalled enterprise resource planning (ERP) implementation problems at Hershey many years ago linked to its order processing problems and significant drops in net income, more recently companies such as Avon and United Airlines have experienced both the unwanted notoriety and the adverse operational and economic impacts of failed or faulty systems. But for every high-profile system failure that is publicized, we believe dozens more are not known to the public. One reason that many of these failures are not known is that the customer frequently has signed up for a transaction that has, in essence, shielded the vendor from any significant accountability and is left with no meaningful remedy resulting from the failure. As a result, the litigation costs of pursuing relief against a vendor that has failed to deliver on its promises often outweigh the likelihood of the customer recovering an amount in excess of the litigation costs from the vendor.

The business case to institute an enterprise information technology management process is both compelling and intuitively sensible. Nevertheless, many companies continue to operate with a diffused and unstructured approach to software licensing and technology services contracting and management. This chapter will provide recommendations that, whether implemented in aggregate or individually, will enhance your processes and outcomes in this area.

The elements of such an enterprise information technology management process include:

- Assessment and modification of the procurement approach;
- Development, implementation, and enforcement of documented practices surrounding critical software licensing issue identification and acceptable resolution;
- Training participants on critical elements of a licensing transaction;
- Controlling the agreement negotiation process; and
- Utilizing tools to extract relevant knowledge, track vendor performance, and enable your enterprise to retrieve and assess the data and otherwise manage its information technology agreements.

The Procurement Process

Typical Process

The typical software request for proposal (RFP) includes several standardized sections detailing instructions for responding to the RFP and includes a general description of the system the company plans to acquire and pages of detailed questions relating to features and functions of the relevant product. If it was also typical for vendors to respond fully and fairly to each of the questions asked in the RFP, relatively little modification of this process would be required. However, most vendors are adept at transforming the legitimate customer-designed vendor capability inquiries included in the RFP process into a vendor marketing exercise.

Responses tend to be very general and are often not responsive to the precise inquiry, or they are responsive with a material qualification. Even follow-up questioning by the customer is not likely to yield responses that are effective in differentiating one vendor from another. Interestingly, in many vendor organizations, the marketing team is the unit with primary responsibility for the RFP content. Frequently the net result of the RFP process does little more than re-package the vendor's marketing material according to the direction of the RFP and simply provide a starting point for pricing negotiations. The typical process can be particularly frustrating to the customer when there are a limited number of vendors with the overall capabilities/product sought, and the customer hopes to use the RFP process to assist it in making a meaningful differentiation among the vendors.

RFP Process Improvement Recommendations

When there is a limited number of vendors with the overall capabilities sought by a customer, we recommend use of a focused process to validate vendor service offerings, pricing, and credentials that we call "Directed Procurement." The Directed Procurement process is designed both to elicit meaningful information for purposes of vendor differentiation and to maintain competition between prospective vendors until the customer obtains the commitments it requires on its key issues so that it can meaningfully enter into an exclusive negotiating period with a preferred vendor or, if it prefers, dual track negotiations with two finalists.

The objectives of the Directed Procurement process are to:

1. Transform the vendor capability inquiry process from a vendor marketing-driven exercise to an effective vendor-differentiating tool;
2. Require focused, relationship-defining questions to be answered by proposed vendor project leads and management—not marketing staff;
3. Focus the procurement process on identification and delivery of customer business objectives; and
4. Obtain written commitments from vendors on key terms and relationship approaches, such as scope of license and license restriction and tying payment to acceptance.

The engine behind the process is the use of targeted questions that require meaningful, substantive responses and that reveal quickly vendors that choose not to or are unable to respond effectively. The customer questions to the vendor are open-ended and require the development of unique responses, rather than yes/no or other canned responses.

Directed Question, Example 1:

- "Based on your experience with implementations of the Software in enterprises comparable to customer, identify the five (5) most significant **technical** problems you are likely to encounter."
- "As to each of the problems, what steps have you used to avoid, mitigate, or resolve the problem?"
- "As to each of the problems, what new process improvements or changes, not discussed above, would you recommend to avoid, mitigate, or resolve the problem?"

Directed Question, Example 2:

Based on your previous experience with similar implementations, describe how you would deliver each of customer's objectives as set forth in Section ____ of the RFP, including responses to the following separately identified sub-questions:

1. What are the typical challenges to completing this activity?
2. What are the corresponding mitigation strategies?
3. What steps can be taken in planning this project to avoid the typical challenges?
4. What involvement (time and types of resources) would be required from customer to successfully complete this task?
5. Can the process you have used in the past to deliver these requirements be improved, and if so, how would you improve it?

In addition, we recommend that the customer include an agreement that it has drafted in the RFP for any software transaction to acquire critical business applications for use across the enterprise (e.g., enterprise resource planning, customer relationship management, financial, human resources, logistics) or other business-critical software procurements in which there are realistic vendor alternatives available to the customer. It is important to note that the customer-based agreement cannot simply be attached to the RFP with a request that the vendor comment, as this approach will likely lead to the vendor simply restating its standard contract positions in response to each issue. Instead, the RFP should include language similar to the following with regard to the customer-drafted agreement:

Required Agreement Instruction:

The Software License Agreement ("Agreement"), attached as Exhibit A, sets forth Customer's required terms and conditions. Customer requires each Vendor either to accept the Agreement affirmatively as presented or to clearly state in writing required modifications, additions, or substitutions (collectively "Exceptions"). Every Vendor must review the Agreement and must set forth *all* Exceptions to the Agreement, if any, in the form of proposed alternative language or identify specific terms to be deleted, and must disclose any impact on the proposed price if Customer rejects the Exceptions. Customer may disqualify and terminate negotiations with any Vendor that did identify an Exception to a given provision in the Agreement in its proposal and subsequently attempts to do so during negotiations. Further, Customer reserves the right to disqualify any Vendor with whom Customer is unable to negotiate a definitive Agreement following notification of intended selection. Therefore, it is in the Vendor's best interest to have the Agreement reviewed by counsel prior to submission of its proposal in response to this RFP. The number and extent of Exceptions to the Agreement will be factored into the evaluation of the Vendor's proposal. *Submission of the Vendor's form Agreement in response to the requirements of this Section of the RFP shall be deemed non-responsive.*

Once a "lead vendor" selection is made, a significant amount of your negotiating leverage as a customer is lost. Therefore, to ensure that the responses are not just part of a vendor strategy to "do what it takes to get to lead vendor status" and to avoid the frequently observed vendor commitment slippage that occurs after RFPs are submitted, the key commitments obtained in this process should be captured in actual contract language and signed off on by an authorized vendor officer before a "lead vendor" is selected. This step is critical to driving value out of the RFP process, avoiding the use of the RFP responses solely as a negotiation starting point, and expediting the overall transaction negotiation cycle.

Depending on the software being procured and the level of information your organization is seeking, the Directed Procurement process can be used by itself or as a supplement to more traditional feature and function inquiries. Regardless of whether you use a more traditional RFP approach or targeted questioning as recommended in connection with the Directed Procurement methodology, staff your evaluation team appropriately, and leave enough time in your schedule to require follow-up responses from the vendor. You deserve to receive useful answers to your questions and can expect to be disappointed with the initial response provided by most vendors.

An Enterprise Approach to Critical Software Licensing Issue Identification and Acceptable Resolution

Typical Process

Many mid-sized to large organizations have a collection of software licenses, loosely "maintained" independently by individuals within the organization who have been involved in such transactions, that may be referred to in connection with future transactions. Some organizations have gone further and have preferred software license language for certain provisions or even template agreements that are to be used in software licensing transactions. But the organization is rare that actually has procedures in place to ensure that its corporate knowledge relating to software licensing, whatever the state of that knowledge, is consistently and systematically applied on behalf of the organization. Even fewer organizations have provided training on best practices for software licensing transactions to the staff charged with managing those transactions. This lack of training often leads company negotiators to argue for wholesale adoption of previously approved form provisions because they do not have an understanding of business rationale behind the provision, nor the confidence or authority to recommend a change.

Unless an organization understands the many business and legal implications each software license transaction presents and has an enterprise approach to handling those issues, it is not possible for its managers and other employees to deliver the best agreement achievable in most circumstances. Given the ability to significantly minimize business risks presented by software licensing transactions and cost savings achievable through a structured approach to such transactions, it is not surprising that companies are increasingly looking for and implementing process improvements in this area.

Process Improvement Recommendations

Enabling your business teams to access, at the point of need in a transaction, relevant business and legal insights and providing training on the meaning and use of those insights to help minimize risks, maximize opportunities, or highlight a need for assistance in connection with software licensing transactions should be the objective of all organizations. While there is no single method that is right for all businesses, the following common ingredients should be included in any effective software licensing issue identification, resolution, and negotiation strategy.

<u>Senior Management Support</u>

Senior management must support the importance to the organization of utilizing effective processes to manage issues surrounding software licensing by:

- Appointing an individual or group to have overall responsibility for approving software license agreements throughout the enterprise with the right to establish and enforce requirements among business units;
- Developing enterprise best-practice software licensing positions and the business rationales supporting those positions, with input throughout the enterprise;
- Providing tools to enable business teams to easily access best-practice positions (Not all transactions carry equal levels of risk, and best-practice positions should take varying levels of risk into account.);
- Providing training to participants in the process on the meaning and use of best-practice positions
- Providing timely support at the point of need to business units trying to implement the enterprise positions; and
- Establishing the expectation that business teams will not materially deviate from best-practice positions unless a manager is prepared to justify an exception request.

Develop Tools

Leading organizations have implemented tools to facilitate the capture and dissemination of knowledge relating to software licensing best practices used in the organization. The tools used vary widely both in content and in sophistication of delivery (e.g., paper-based to interactive) from organization to organization and include issue checklists, agreement libraries, form provisions, template agreements, annotated agreements, and extranet-based knowledge delivery tools.

Checklists: Checklists can provide an easy and effective method to spread best practices when they are focused on single subjects (e.g., security diligence checklist) and are combined with discussions of the business issues that each item on the list is intended to address. For example, if a security checklist identifies a requirement for the vendor to permit penetration testing, the business reason supporting this enhanced level of protection should also be included (e.g., because we are a heavily regulated industry and are subject to high levels of accountability for the security of our customer's data, whether or not it is in our immediate control, we require vendors that will store customer data on their servers to commit to allowing us to conduct penetration testing both to meet our diligence obligations and to test the vendor's commitment to security within its organization). Finally, checklists that require affirmation of compliance with the subject matter directives in the checklist and approval of any material deviations by the designated oversight officer or group are far more effective at causing enterprise behavior to conform to those requirements.

Agreement libraries, form provisions, and template agreements: These tools vary from collections of agreements and agreement fragments maintained in the desk drawers of individual employees to databases searchable by type of agreement, vendor, or type of provision with links to PDF versions of the relevant agreements and amendments. With regard to form provisions and template agreements, just as in the case of checklists, discussions of the business issues relevant to the documents promote their effective use by your business teams. Thus, we favor annotated agreements that provide knowledge content with the template agreement. An example of a section from an annotated agreement from our technology contracting knowledge tool called KnowledgeGate™ follows:

Section 3.1 – License Grant

Use Note

The best license for Customer to obtain is the broadest license; one that enables the use of the Software across the Customer enterprise and by all users authorized by Customer, including employees, both in their offices and at home (if applicable), and all affiliated entities and their employees.

In some instances, the parties will negotiate for some software products to be licensed on a perpetual basis (best for Customer) and other(s) to be licensed on a term basis (better for Licensor). In such a circumstance, the parties must clearly define the products in each category.

The language in Section 3.1 (License Grant), which is not bracketed, provides for the ideal license from Customer's standpoint. However, it may be difficult or prohibitively expensive to achieve this scope of license, so the bracketed portion, which creates a "Concurrent User" license, may be required. By licensing the software on a Concurrent User basis, the Licensor is assured that as there is growth in the number of users, it will receive additional payment.

Many Licensor licenses are written in terms of allowing the Customer to use the software for "its internal purposes only." Such a restriction will likely not encompass all of the uses to which the Customer may want to put the software. A better, more encompassing approach is to draft the license in terms of permitting the Customer to use the software for "its business purposes."

1. License Grant

[Perpetual License Example] Licensor grants to Customer and its Users a perpetual, non-exclusive license to use the Licensed Software for Customer's and its Users' business activities *[subject to the Concurrent User requirements, if any, of this Agreement.]*

[Term License Example] For those items of Licensed Software identified in Exhibit B (Licensed Software) as "Term Applications," Licensor grants to Customer and its Users a non-exclusive license to use such items of Licensed Software for Customer's and its Users' business activities for the periods identified in Exhibit B (Licensed Software). *[Such license shall be subject to any Concurrent User limitations set forth in Exhibit B].*

Provide Support

The business teams that are responsible for implementing technology within the organization may be accountable to managers who place conflicting demands on the team. The manager of the business unit sponsoring the acquisition of software may be placing pressure on those negotiating the license to "just get it done so we can start implementation." At the same time, legal or procurement may be demanding that certain steps be followed or contract concessions be obtained, with much less sensitivity to the project time impacts.

This type of conflict rarely leads to the best overall solution for the organization and can frustrate efforts to develop effective licensing management solutions across the enterprise. To minimize such conflicts, it is important that the business team charged with implementing the organization's licensing best practices is also provided with timely support from legal and other departments so that both the organization's project timeline and its licensing management objectives can be met.

The payoff to your organization of harnessing, distributing, and applying relevant licensing knowledge can be significant. Use the suggestions above to get started and improve your licensing outcomes.

Controlling the Agreement Negotiation Process

Typical Process

Frequently, software vendors drive the negotiation process beginning with the often successful vendor insistence on using its standard agreement and exhibits to control the agenda and scheduling of negotiation sessions. Vendors will be pleased to put critical issues on which the parties differ in the "parking lot" and continue to negotiate the less controversial terms. The more time and effort spent by the customer on the less controversial issues, the more committed the customer becomes to that vendor's solution, and as time passes, the vendor knows that the customer has few realistic options. Not surprisingly, at the end of the line, when the tough "parking lot" issues are addressed, the customer will observe much less vendor flexibility toward the resolution of these issues.

Further, because the customer starts with the vendor agreements, every change to the agreement during negotiations appears to be a vendor "concession." In reality, these "concessions" are simple, incremental movements toward fairness. And because of the magnitude of change to a vendor standard agreement needed to achieve fairness, the customer is inclined to be overly selective of the issues to negotiate to avoid prolonging negotiations. Finally, because negotiation sessions are not structured, much time can be wasted, causing key individuals on the customer team to be less likely to remain committed to participation in the process.

Process Improvement Recommendations

Our experience with software licensing projects demonstrates that requiring directed and concentrated effort from all project participants, from kick-off to conclusion, will result in the customer achieving its business objectives in the most cost-efficient and expedient manner. Assuming a customer-drafted agreement was included in the RFP, as recommended in our discussion of the procurement process, your internal negotiation team discussions should focus on the identification and internal resolution of key business issues and your desired contract requirements as to those issues.

We often refer to this grouping of issues, which usually number around a dozen, as the customer's "Tier 1" issues. The Tier 1 issues, which may include issues such as scope of license, payment methodology, and vendor accountability, should be the focus of the initial negotiations. We use the Tier 1 issues to drive the initial negotiation agendas. These issues should be brought to resolution (approved contract language should be signed off on by both parties) before proceeding with the other, and far more numerous, transaction issues. This approach presents the customer with viable business options in the event the vendors seek to leverage their "lead vendor" position too aggressively. By raising these issues and requiring resolution at the outset, the vendors know the customer is not yet irreversibly committed to the transaction, and that should create additional leverage to move the vendors closer to the customer's preferred positions.

We highly recommend that the customer set a formalized agenda for each negotiation session. We have found that such agendas serve to focus the negotiation efforts and underscore to the vendor that the customer is in control of the process. Of course, the degree of control over the process will vary with the type of transaction and the culture of the customer organization. Below is an example of negotiation directions to a vendor that reflect a desire by the customer to have a high degree of control and a very structured process in negotiations relating to a mission-critical system. While this example may be a bit "over the top" for the typical transaction, we feel the concepts are instructive and can be easily modified and adapted to suit your needs.

Negotiation Structure Directive

To accomplish the timing and business objectives of Customer in connection with this licensing transaction, Customer requires a structured negotiation process. To that end, it is required that Vendor has decision makers and their proposed lead project executive in attendance at all negotiation sessions. Customer intends to pursue negotiations on a daily basis, excluding, to the extent possible, weekends from [insert dates].

An agenda for each session will be circulated by Customer no later than the Thursday before the upcoming week of negotiations. The agenda will identify the issues to be addressed during the sessions and provide specific references to the Customer agreement or RFP sections that state Customer's position on the issues. No later than 12 p.m. PST on the Sunday before the negotiation sessions, Vendor will provide a written description of any issues it has with the concepts advanced by Customer on the specific issues for that week's agenda. It is critical that Vendor's comments remain focused on the identification of, and reasons underlying, any conceptual issues (e.g., "This provision is unfair to Vendor because ..."; or "This is acceptable, provided it is adjusted to address our concern that [state specifics] ..."). Specific language changes should be provided only in addition to, and not as a substitute for, identifying the conceptual issue and articulating the reasons underlying the issue. To the extent the parties agree to change any conceptual issue, language modifications will be made by the Customer negotiating team and submitted to Vendor for validation.

Negotiation sessions will be structured to focus on discussion and resolution of the conceptual issues identified by Vendor. Areas of disagreement will be tracked, and after a pre-determined time, the parties will move to the next agenda item. There will be separate negotiating team caucuses as appropriate to finalize resolution of open agenda issues. The deliverable from each team arising from such caucuses will be to bring forward its proposed resolution on the open issues being discussed. Negotiating teams will again try to reach resolution on these issues, and, if unsuccessful, escalation plans will be developed.

An ongoing issues list will be maintained by Customer, and owners of each resolution task will be identified. The owners will be responsible for reporting on progress per the resolution plan. It is the intent of Customer not to move on to new issues until all issues on an existing agenda are closed or deemed to be on a meaningful resolution path, and not simply being deferred.

While no single process must be used to structure your negotiations, our preferred approach is to start with Tier 1 issues, obtain detailed vendor comments to the customer-proposed Agreement, and then work issues to resolution to minimize commitment slippage and issue reopening. Take control of the negotiation process. Your doing so will lead to a more efficient and effective negotiation and will leave no doubt with the vendor that you are a sophisticated, informed, and prepared buyer.

Managing Completed Software Licenses

Typical Process

Organizations of all sizes commonly have no system to

1. Capture important information from their completed software licenses, such as annual costs and maintenance renewal dates,
2. Collect and retrieve the actual software license terms,
3. Track performance issues, and
4. Extract knowledge from existing licensing transactions for use in future transactions.

Frequently, the final version of a licensing agreement remains in the hands of the employee to whom the signed agreement was delivered. Companies often cannot even find agreements more than a year after they are entered into. Should the typical company need to examine the terms of all or a group of its existing licensing agreements in connection with a software licensing audit, a sale of its business or business line, or an outsourcing, it will experience limited success, even after devoting substantial internal efforts to the cause.

The absence of a system to store and retrieve the actual agreements almost ensures the inability of the organization to effectively track compliance by the vendor with the terms of the agreements and the ability to track and resolve performance issues efficiently. This is not likely as significant a problem in instances in which an organization is simply signing standard vendor agreements because, as discussed in earlier chapters, there are few vendor obligations and even fewer tools for the customer to meaningfully manage issues that arise included in such agreements.

However, as your organization progresses in its capabilities with regard to software licensing, it is essential to have a process in place to enable ongoing evaluations of vendor performance and agreement compliance. In the absence of such a system, it can be expected that over time, hard fought agreement concessions obtained during the negotiation process will be forgotten or ignored, and standard vendor practices will be reverted to in their place.

Process Improvement Recommendations

It is not expensive, time-consuming, or complicated to implement a process to assist your organization in effectively managing its licensing and other information technology agreements, provide a basic level of education to your business teams on critical issues, enable your company to easily retrieve agreements and amendments, and identify and mitigate risks. There are a number of commercially available tools to enable effective capture of key data about your software licensing agreements, as well as the agreements themselves.

To fast-track improvement in your organization regarding its management of software licenses and related technology agreements, you will need to:

- Appoint an individual or group to have overall responsibility for managing software license agreements throughout the enterprise (this should be the same individual or group responsible for approving such agreements, as discussed above);
- Develop a mechanism for collecting, cataloging, and storing your software licenses (A filing cabinet is better than no process; however, a simple database or commercial product may better serve your objectives.);
- Commit resources to review, at a minimum, the agreements for key events and dates, vendor commitments, and cost and pricing. Ideally, these resources could also extract information on how the agreements your organization is actually executing compare to your established best-practice approaches to such agreements; and
- Create a simple report card for monitoring vendor performance in key areas such as meeting implementation dates, complying with service levels, and adherence to agreement terms.

If implemented, the above processes, like others discussed in this book, will assist your organization in effectively controlling costs, improving your corporate knowledge and capabilities in structuring license agreements, and identifying and minimizing business risks inherent in such transactions.

Appendices

APPENDIX A

CROSS-REFERENCE OF CHAPTER DISCUSSION OF VENDOR LICENSE PROVISIONS

As an aid to the reader, we have compiled the following cross-reference of chapters in which specific provisions of the vendor form are discussed.

Vendor Form License Section	Chapter
1.3 (Definition of Licensed Software)	3
2.1 (License Grant)	3
2.2 (Licensed Software Use Restrictions)	3
2.11 (Audit)	3
5 (Fees and Payments)	3
1.4 (Definition of Documentation)	4
2.7 (Delivery)	4
7 (Limited Warranties)	5
8 (Disclaimer of Warranties)	5
9 (Limitation of Liability)	5
11 (Indemnity)	5
6 (Confidentiality)	6
3 (Support and Maintenance)	7
1 (Definitions)	8
2.5 (Ownership)	8
2.6 (Feedback)	8
2.10 (Aggregated Data)	8
11.3 (Limitation of Actions)	8
17 (Entire Agreement)	8
19 (Assignment)	8
24 (Publicity)	8

APPENDIX B

INTERNET RESOURCES

Many excellent resources are available on the Internet regarding software licensing. We have identified some of the more useful sites in the following table.

Web Site	Description
www.efoley.com	Home page for Foley & Lardner's eFOLEY website, a business resource focused on delivering practical content from a wide range of subject matter experts targeted at common business issues arising from the use and development of technology.
KnowledgeGate™ (accessed through www.efoley.com)	Subscription-based technology agreement best-practice knowledge base and extranet-based technology agreement management tools.
www.gao.gov (Special Projects/GAO Best Practices Work/Information Technology)	Collection of whitepapers on information technology best practices commissioned by the federal government.
http://www.sei.cmu.edu/pub/documents/02.reports/pdf/02tr010.pdf	PDF detailing the requirements of the Carnegie-Mellon Software Engineering Institute's Software Acquisition Capability Maturity Model® (SA-CMM®) detailing useful methodologies to address the issues discussed in Chapter 9.
http://www.don-imit.navy.mil/esi/uploaded_documents/0210YZX17644.pdf	Department of Defense whitepaper titled "Best Practices For Enterprise Software Agreements."

Web Site	Description
http://www.epic.org/privacy/privacy_resources_faq.html	Website sponsored by the Electronic Privacy Information Center aggregating Internet resources addressing data privacy issues.
www.gnu.org	Home of the GNU Project, creator of the GNU General Public License and GNU Lesser General Public License. The GNU Project is sponsored primarily by the Free Software Foundation.
www.tuxedo.org/~esr/writings/cathedral-bazaar/	Eric Raymond's famous book setting forth the case for open source.
http://tuxedo.org/~esr/writings/magic-cauldron/	Eric Raymond's white paper on revenue models for open source software.
http://softwaredev.earthweb.com/sdopen	Information for software developers regarding open source.
www.acl.lanl.gov/publications/OpenSourceHPC-v17.html	The Case for Open Source Software Development for Scalable High Performance Computing

APPENDIX C

GLOSSARY OF KEY SOFTWARE LICENSING TERMS

Application programming interface: Abbreviated API. Information relating to how software communicates with the operating system and other programs, including file formats, data export capabilities, etc. The API is generally essential to writing interfaces and other programs that interact with and exchange information with the software.

ASCII: Abbreviation for American Standard Code for Information Interchange. An almost universally accepted format for exchanging text-based information. ASCII format is, however, limited in that it does not preserve the formatting of the text or any special characteristics of the document (e.g., footnotes, tables, bullet points).

Backups: Duplicate copies of data, generally stored at an off-site, secure facility.

Central processing unit: Abbreviated CPU. The portion of a computer that controls the processing and storage of data.

Client computer: A personal computer or workstation connected to a network file server. *See* **file server**.

Client-server network: A type of network in which server computers provide files to client computers. *See* **client** computer and **file server**.

Consequential damages: Consequential damages are damages that indirectly result from a breach of contract. This type of damages includes lost profits, damage to data, damage to business reputation, etc. Consequential damages are sometimes called "incidental," "indirect," or "special" damages.

Core: Early on, a CPU had only a single central processing unit (or "core") on it. To increase performance, additional cores, or CPUs, were added. For example, a dual-core CPU has two central processing units, so it appears to the operating system as two CPUs. Different software can be running on each core simultaneously or a particular task the computer is working on divided between or among the cores. The use of additional cores can greatly increase the overall power, speed, and efficiency of the computer in which they reside.

Direct damages: Direct damages are those damages that directly result from a breach of contract. This type of damages includes, for example, the fees paid to the vendor under the agreement.

Enterprise: The collection of entities comprising a particular business (e.g., all affiliates, subsidiaries, joint ventures, and other related companies).

File: A collection of data or information stored under a specified name on a disk. Examples of files are programs, data files, spreadsheets, databases, and word-processing documents.

File server: A central computer used to store files (e.g., data, word-processing documents, programs) for use by client computers connected to a network. Most file servers run special operating systems known as network operating systems (NOSs). Novell Netware and Windows NT are common NOSs. *See* **client computer** and **client-server network**.

Implementation: The process by which software is made ready for use on a particular licensee's systems.

Indemnity: An obligation of a party to protect the other party to a contract from certain types of claims by third parties. The primary indemnity provided by vendors in software license agreements is the obligation to protect the licensee from claims by third parties alleging the software infringes their intellectual property rights.

License grant: The language in a license agreement that defines the license being granted to the licensee. For example, "Licensor hereby grants Licensee a perpetual, non-exclusive license to use the Licensed Software for its internal business purposes."

Licensee: The person or entity that is licensing a particular software application from a licensor.

Licensor: The person or entity that is licensing a particular software application to others.

Limitation of liability: A clause found in most software license agreements limiting one or both parties' liability for damages. Most limitations of liability are divided into two parts: an exclusion of all liability for consequential damages and an overall cap on direct and all other types of damages. This cap is typically set at all or some portion of the license fees paid for the software.

Local area network: Abbreviated LAN. A network of computers and other devices generally located within a relatively limited area (e.g., within a particular office, building, or group of buildings).

Object code: The machine-readable version of a computer program. *See* **source code**.

Open source software: Software that is distributed under a license that promotes continued development and free use of the program. Open source software is typically distributed without any warranties, indemnities, or other contractual protections. Such software is essentially provided as-is to the licensee.

Service bureau: Generally refers to a licensee's use of software for the benefit of unrelated third parties—for example, using an accounts payable accounting application to process the data of businesses that are completely unrelated to the original licensee.

Shrink-Wrap: Refers to a pre-printed form license agreement packaged or otherwise furnished with a piece of software. The license is generally presented as non-negotiable. It originally described licenses that were packaged with the software documentation and wrapped in cellophane (i.e., shrink-wrapped).

Source code: The version of a computer program that can be read by humans. The source code is translated into machine-readable code by a program called a "compiler." Access to the source code is required to understand how a computer program works or to modify the program. *See* **object code**.

Term license: A license in which the licensee may use the software for only a defined period, typically one to five years.

Vendor: The person or entity that is licensing a particular software application to others.

Virtual machine: A computer made of software. This software computer operates in much the same way as a physical computer. It runs an operating system and applications. Depending on its configuration, a single physical computer can be set up to run multiple virtual machines. Each virtual machine may be seen as a separate, stand-alone computer, even though it has no physical presence.

Wide area network: Abbreviated WAN. A network of computers and other devices distributed over a broad geographic area.

Workstation: A personal computer connected to a network. A workstation can also refer to a high-performance computer used for intensive graphics or numerical calculations.

ABOUT THE AUTHORS

Michael R. Overly is a partner in the e-Business & Information Technology Group in the Los Angeles office of Foley & Lardner LLP. As an attorney, a Certified Information Systems Security Professional (CISSP), and a former electrical engineer, he focuses his practice on counseling clients regarding technology licensing, information security, electronic commerce, and Internet and multimedia law.

Mr. Overly writes and speaks frequently on the legal issues of doing business on the Internet, technology in the workplace, e-mail, and electronic evidence. He has written numerous articles on these subjects and has authored chapters in several treatises. He is the author of the best-selling e-policy, HOW TO DEVELOP COMPUTER, E-MAIL, AND INTERNET GUIDELINES TO PROTECT YOUR COMPANY AND ITS ASSETS (AMACOM 1998), THE OPEN SOURCE HANDBOOK (Pike & Fischer 2003), OVERLY ON ELECTRONIC EVIDENCE (West Publishing 2002), and DOCUMENT RETENTION IN THE ELECTRONIC WORKPLACE (Pike & Fischer 2001). Mr. Overly can be reached at moverly@foley.com.

James R. Kalyvas is a partner in the Los Angeles office of Foley & Lardner LLP. Chair of the firm's e-Business & Information Technology Group, he is a member of the firm's Intellectual Property Department. Mr. Kalyvas advises companies, public entities, and associations on the procurement, negotiation, and implementation of information technology. He specializes in structuring technology and business process outsourcing transactions, multi-vendor sourcing strategies, and enterprise resource planning initiatives. He has incorporated his experience in handling billions of dollars of technology transactions into the development of several proprietary tools relating to the effective management of the technology procurement and implementation processes.

Mr. Kalyvas is a frequent commentator and speaker on technology trends, enterprise information system strategies, outsourcing, and technology business partner relationships. Mr. Kalyvas can be reached at jkalyvas@foley.com.

ASPATORE